"Debbie did an amazing job through her story of portraying the barriers to accessing mental health care. Her story paints an accurate picture of the roller coaster that many families feel they can never get off of, while on the journey to recovery with their loved ones. Her family story is one of resiliency even in incredibly difficult times. Had the family had psychoeducational resources then that we have now, maybe the outcome would have been different."

-Lacey Berumen, Phd-c, MNM
Executive Director, NAMI Colorado

"Debbie Nau Redmond has written a personal and painful account of the terrible toll that mental illness takes on individuals and on their families. More importantly, this retelling of the love and affection that her family shared as they struggled with an ongoing tragedy is a powerful reminder of the strength of family bonds. This is an important read for anyone struggling with these issues."

-Steven W. Jackson, MSW, LCSW

"Silent Voices is an emotionally charged and engaging novel… This is a personal story inspired by true events and real people in Redmond's life. Well done, Debbie Nau Redmond! By writing this story so beautifully, you have truly done your family proud and have inspired us readers simultaneously. Outstanding!"

-Rita V., Readers Favorite

"Mental illness is perhaps the most misunderstood thing in today's society. "Silent Voices: The True Story Of One Family's Tragedy and Journey Toward Acceptance, Grace, and Forgiveness" is the memoir of Debbie Nau Redmond as she recollects the tragedy of her brother's schizophrenia and the severe impact it had on her family. Wishing for greater understanding of schizophrenia and other severe mental illness, "Silent Voices" is a much needed read for those who want to truly understand mental illness and all its problems."

-Carol Logan, Midwest Book Review

SILENT VOICES

A true story of one family's tragedy and journey toward acceptance, grace and forgiveness

DEBBIE NAU REDMOND

Library of Congress Control Number: 2014921770
ISBN-13: 978-0-9862259-0-1

Silent Voices soft-cover edition 2015
Printed in the United States of America
First Edition: April 2011

Book cover by Deborah Bradseth of Tugboat Design
Editors: Julie Pinkerton, Katherine Mayfield and Mike Valentino

Published by: Aspenglo, LLC.
Website: www.debbieredmond.com

Acknowledgments

To My Husband Charlie: God blessed me with you and I am sincerely grateful. Thank you for encouraging me to follow my dream. I appreciate all your love, support and friendship! You're the best!

To My Family: Thank you for all your love, support and understanding on why I needed to write this book.

To My Friends: Thank you for all your kindness, suggestions and support in writing this book. You are all wonderful friends and my life is more enriched having you in it.

Dedications

To My Parents: It takes a lot of courage and strength to stand by your child when they are ill. I admire you for all of your love, support, strength and faith. No parent should experience what you did. I'm sorry for all the pain you have endured. Thank you for supporting me with this book. I feel very blessed to have you as my parents.

To My Siblings Gene, Theresa, Jeff and Charlie: I'm so proud of you. You pulled yourselves through a rough and difficult situation with character and your heads held high. I know this book will reopen some old feelings. I hope and prayer you take this negative situation and make it something positive in your lives.

To Carol M: No words can express my sincere gratitude. Thank you for helping my family. You have more courage than anyone I know.

To My Brother Ricky: Thank you. If it weren't for you, I would not be the person I am today. You taught me a level of spirituality, understanding and compassion that I would have never known. I hope your story will help others.

To My Brothers Jim and Bruce: Not a day goes by that you don't cross my mind or I feel a sense of sadness. You will always be in my heart, my mind and my soul. You are tremendously missed for what was and what could have been. I will always love you and you will never be forgotten.

Finally, to all the "Silent Voices": To those parents/family members who have children with Schizophrenia, may the doctors hear your voices and give you help. To all the people with Schizophrenia, may God bless your journey and may your voices be heard.

Table of Contents

Something is Not Quite Right

I t was Thursday, September 29, 1983, and I woke up completely exhausted. The sun was shining but it felt gloomy to me. I hadn't had much sleep the last week. My family was experiencing a tsunami of turmoil and confusion, and we were so drained from facing the threat of violence. I felt sick to my stomach, not like the flu, but like you know in your heart that something is terribly wrong. I knew I had to go to school, regardless of how I felt.

It was the beginning of my senior year in high school, and it was our homecoming weekend. I had practice all week for cheerleading, and preparing for the parade and football game. I was also busy painting posters and locker tags for all the sporting events. Everyone was excited about the parties and the dance, except for me. I had no desire to be a part of any of these activities.

As I was driving to school, tears rolled down my face. I did not know why I was crying; all I knew was I felt a deep sense of loss. I remember the song "Total Eclipse of the Heart" by Bonnie Tyler was playing on the radio, which I think added to my tears. Maybe it was dealing with my family's difficulties that was getting to me or maybe knowing it was my senior year homecoming weekend and

I was completely disconnected from everyone. I was not enjoying any of it! Great! Welcome to a wonderful senior year.

I got to school and sat in my classes all morning staring at the clock. I was so thankful it was only a half-day of school for me. When I got out around noon, I felt light-headed, my hands were shaky and I had a terrible stomach ache all morning. I did not hear one thing that any of the teachers said. All I knew was I wanted to get home because I felt a strange need to be there. A deep feeling of fear swept over me. I needed to be home to protect my family. I was supposed to stay at school all afternoon to paint some more posters, but to be honest I didn't care. I just knew I had to leave, so I left quickly.

I got home around 12:15. My brothers Jim, 32, Ricky, 22, Charlie, 21, and Bruce, 20, were home. Jim was visiting from Seattle and Bruce was home because his first day of work was canceled, which was good, because he'd only recently returned home from the hospital and was still getting over a bad case of viral meningitis. Charlie was downstairs getting ready to go to his job at a retail shop.

For some reason, Jim was acting very anxious and nervous. I asked him, "What's wrong?"

With a worried look, he said, "I don't know, something seems wrong, and I have a bad feeling."

Me too! I agreed and told him, "I felt sick to my stomach all morning, and I know it's not the flu."

Jim, Bruce and I watched TV for a little while, as I tried to eat something. I don't remember what we were watching — my mind was somewhere else. I just could not shake the weird, negative and fearful feelings I was experiencing. I decided that I needed to lie down; maybe it would help my queasy stomach and calm me down. As I was walking to my bedroom, I noticed my brother Ricky out in the backyard asleep on the lawn chair. He looked ghostly white, as though there was no life in him. A strong chill raised the hair on the back of my neck. I called for my brother Bruce to come to the dining room glass door and we both watched Ricky sleeping. For a quiet moment, we stared intensely to see if, in fact, he was breathing. His chest rose and fell at a very slow pace one moment, then it would start pumping erratically the next. It seemed really strange, not at all like normal breathing.

"He looks weird... something isn't right," I said wearily. Suddenly, I ordered, "Lock the door — and keep it locked!"

My brother did what I told him. As I was standing there watching Ricky, a deep sense of sadness overcame me. Memories started flooding back into my mind of all the fun times we had as kids. So much had changed with Ricky and my family over the last two years. The constant turmoil and confusion kept fear brewing between us. With the intense stress the family had all but reached its breaking point.

I started to drift back to a time of sweet, wonderful family memories, when things were good and Ricky was a joy to be around.

CHAPTER ONE

Sweet Memories Brings Joy

As I think back about family, my mind fills up with so many sweet memories. I grew up in an average middle-class family. We didn't have a white-picket fence, but pretty darn close. I was born in Littleton, Colorado. There are eight children in our family. It's not hard to figure out. Yes, we are Catholic; yes, we almost filled up a whole church pew. We made a lot of commotion when we sat down, us kids fighting about who was going to sit by who, while my parents were hushing us to be quiet. This was a Sunday ritual. I have six brothers (Jim, Gene, Jeff, Ricky, Charlie and Bruce) and one sister (Theresa) — all born in a fifteen-year span.

I'm so grateful I came from a large family. Days were never boring, and I always had someone to play with. I loved my family. We usually got along, and we always had a good time with each other, playing games, watching

Top L to R: Jim, Theresa, Jeff, Gene
Bottom L to R: Debbie, Charlie, Ricky, Bruce

Top L to R: Jeff, Theresa
Middle L to R: Gene, Ricky, Jim
Bottom L to R: Bruce, Debbie, Charlie

Top L to R: Charlie, Ricky, Jeff, Theresa, Gene, Jim
Bottom L to R: Bruce, Debbie, Mom, Dad

cartoons or running around outside. The only thing I did not like was that it was always loud with kids yelling, and the TV/music blaring. If I did not speak fast, yell or cut in, I would not be heard, because we all tend to speak and laugh at the same time. I also had to fight for my food. Sitting at the dinner table, if I did not move fast enough or be aggressive with grabbing food, my brothers would eat it all, like hungry savages — and I would starve to death. Well, that's what I thought anyway.

I am the youngest of the kids. I'm sure some of my brothers and my sister would say I was spoiled. I don't think I was, because I was always grateful for what I had and I was very grounded in what was important in life and what was not. I just happened to have the luck of being born last when finances were getting better for my parents — and their parenting skills became much more relaxed (probably because they got tired of all these kids not listening). Childhood was a much tougher time for my older siblings. My parents were saving every nickel. They lived in a small three-bedroom house, as they were just getting by. My dad was an engineer associate for Western Electric in Omaha, Nebraska. He worked long hours and a lot of overtime to keep food on the table. Before I was born, my dad asked to be transferred to Denver with Western Electric. My parents came to Colorado for their honeymoon and fell in love with the mountains. When my dad's company had a job opportunity become available in Denver, he jumped on it and they moved to Littleton in 1964. Most of his career his salary was only in the mid-$20,000 range, which was not much for eight kids. I do not know how he did it, but he did — and I do not remember my dad ever complaining. No matter how tight money was, he always tried to provide the best he could to give us nice, new school clothes and pay for activities and sports.

My dad was also a very good handyman. I can hardly recall my parents calling a repairman to come fix things. He managed to fix and repair whatever was broken in our house. I'm not sure if that was always good! Even though he worked very long hours, he found time on the weekends to repair household items, take us on adventurous mountain picnics and hikes, or come to our sporting events.

Top L to R: Gene, Theresa, Jim
Bottom L to R: Jeff, Ricky, Debbie, Bruce, Charlie and our dog Shadow

My mom, on the other hand, would always help save a nickel by sitting at the kitchen table sewing or repairing our torn or worn out play clothes or handing down our clothes from one kid to the other. She saved every brown paper bag from the grocery store and washed all aluminum foil for reuse. I was very lucky; my mom was wonderful and I considered her a "supermom." A stay-home

Mom and Dad

mom until I got into high school, she had the house clean and dinner ready at six o'clock sharp! She kept us kids organized from one sport to another, rushing around the house, and driving fast to make sure we were not late for practices or games. She supported us in all of our extra activities and escorted us to our various sporting events, including football, hockey, soccer, baseball, track, softball or gymnastics just to name a few. Even though she was busy keeping us ding-a-ling kids clean and out of trouble, over the years she still managed to take care of two dogs, two cats, four litters of kittens, a couple of birds, a few hamsters, a turtle and a chipmunk, all with a smile on her face.

My mom was also very creative and painted ceramics, organized flower arrangements and developed some type of wall hangings to decorate our house. During her extra time late at night, while we were sleeping, she managed to crochet or sew some type of clothing project. Even though money was tight, our house looked clean and nice — and we were dressed in a presentable manner.

Family Picnic
L to R: Bruce, Debbie, Jeff, Ricky, Charlie

Family Picnic
L to R: Theresa, Debbie, Ricky, Bruce, Jeff, Charlie

I have lots of great memories from childhood. Quite often my parents took us on fun-filled picnics to the mountains. We would venture out to new areas somewhere along the front range of Colorado. Somehow, we managed to find something interesting to do or to explore from rough dirt roads that lead to ghost towns or cabins, climbing up rocks and trees, or even discovering old dirty mine shafts. There was never a dull moment. There were many funny times like when my parents stopped at the gas station to fill up and my brother Jeff went to the bathroom without telling anyone. As my parents drove away, we all giggled and waved goodbye to my brother out the back window, as he was running after us, waving and screaming for us to stop. After a few minutes, with all the kids laughing, my parents realized they forgot a kid, and turned around to go back to get him. Lesson learned: count your kids before driving off!

Another nice memory was when we drove down to Monument, Colorado and we were exploring a new dirt road that lead to a mountain area called Devil's Head for a family picnic. As we were driving up the dirt road, it started to rain hard, and the road had become very slick and muddy. My mom saw a little baby chipmunk roll down the side of the hill by the road. The rain was coming down so strongly it was basically washing the chipmunk away. My mom made my dad stop, and she got out of the car with her coat over her head and ran to the chipmunk to save it. She gently picked it up and brought the baby chipmunk back into the car. She wrapped it in a dishcloth to keep it dry and safe, so we could bring it home. We got to have a pet chipmunk named "Chippy" all summer until it was healthy enough to go back into the wild. We now refer to this road as "Chipmunk Road," and we still today go up that road for picnics.

Our Pet Chipmunk
L to R: Jeff, Chippy and Charlie

My family mostly enjoyed outdoor activities such as camping, hiking and four-wheeling (jeeping). We were

Jeeping at Mt. Antero
L to R: Dad, Ricky, Bruce, Debbie, Charlie,
Theresa, and of course, the dog

Camping & Jeeping to a Lake
Top L to R: Mom, Charlie
Bottom L to R: Ricky, Debbie, Bruce and
Shadow

definitely an outdoor family. Actually, we still are. One of our favorite spots to visit is Buena Vista, Colorado; it's a beautiful place with pine trees, blue lakes, rushing rivers, high rugged mountain peaks and white chalk cliffs. There are lots of camping spots, hiking trails, mountain climbing and jeep trails. This area provided us with so many fun memories. Our Jeep got banged up or scratched on the rough roads; my brother caught tons of fish; we explored deep mine shafts; we found cool gems and crystals; our family almost got hit by lightning on top of a mountain; and bears frequently walked through our campsite.

There is a particular campground called Cascade Campground located up the mountain valley by Princeton Hot Springs. This campground was our favorite place to go. As kids, my mom made us go play while she did the camping chores and cooked dinner over the campfire. In one of the campsites, we built paths all over the hillside with white rocks. We would play tag, and you would have to stay within the path or you would be out. We built the paths over forty years ago, and I am proud to say the majority of them are still there today. There are spots where other people have added rocks over the years. It makes me laugh whenever I go there to visit. Who would have thought a simple game we created for a weekend would last a lifetime.

Whenever I look back at our family camping pictures, the sadness and shadows fade for a moment. We four-wheeled and hiked; we climbed mountains and hillsides; and we camped and explored many areas all over Colorado. Camping was not only an adventure, but also an education. My mom was always teaching us about the history of the ghost towns, the different types of wild flowers or plants, the history of the Jeep roads, and the different types of gems and rocks. I feel very blessed that our parents taught us the joy and love of the mountains. I can't even imagine our lives without going to the mountains for a weekend adventure.

The majority of the time the oldest four kids would play or hang out together, and us younger four would play together. There was no fighting or bickering except when we played backyard sports, kick-the-can or the game Risk. Someone would always be accused of cheating by

Our Rock Path
Cascade Campground

Camping - Exploring a Cabin
Top L to R: Charlie, Bruce
Bottom L to R: Ricky, Dad, Shadow, Debbie

A Game of Risk
Front L to R: Ricky, Charlie
Back L to R: Jim, Jeff, Gene, Debbie

Gene and Ricky playing hockey in our backyard

kicking the "can" early or adding an extra "army man" onto the Risk board. Overall, I honestly can say we all got along extremely well. This is shocking considering all the different personalities.

My mom did an excellent job of keeping us in line and making sure we all played well together. She also made sure we each had our own activity that we enjoyed doing from Boy Scouts, playing music, to different sporting activities. However, I think the one *love* we all share was the enjoyment of the mountains.

Overall, I can't complain and I had a wonderful childhood. I grew up in a neighborhood full of kids. We all rode bikes and played tag or hide-and-seek. My brothers always protected and played with me. My family ate dinner together in the evenings and we were never late because you would miss out on all the good food. The TV was turned off, we said the dinner prayer, and we all sat at the table to eat together. We supported each other and we were there for each other when needed. We played well together — and most importantly, we liked each other.

But don't get me wrong; we were not perfect nor were we the "Cleavers." Like most kids, there were times when we drove our parents crazy, did things we were not supposed to do, acted like snotty little brats, and even had neighbors complain about us here and there. Usually the neighbors would complain to my mom that we were too loud, ran across their flowers, kicked the ball into their window, and of course, rang their doorbell and ran. I have to admit, most of it was true.

Discipline was always an action, maybe a hard hand here

and there, but never a lack of love. Personally, I still can't believe my parents are not bald from all the things their eight kids put them through: broken bones, bad grades, unexplained absences, teasing neighborhood kids, playing loud music, "tee-peeing" the neighborhood, getting into car fender benders, talking back, throwing parties, and missing curfew… just to name a few.

So as you can see, we were the "typical" middle-class American family… at least I thought we were until my mind drifted back to my brother Ricky.

CHAPTER TWO

So Much Love and Admiration…
So Much Potential

A s my mind continues to drift back to all the wonderful memories, especially with my brother Ricky, it brings a warm smile to my face and my sadness begins to fade. Ricky was number five in the order of kids and was full of energy. He was very independent and adventurous. When

Ricky

we were little playing games around the house or playing with the neighborhood kids, Ricky was always the leader. He came up with interesting twists to the rules of the games, for instance, you could only stand or hide in certain areas of the yard; or you could not step on a crack in the drive way when you came up to kick-the-can. He had this aura or energy that attracted people to him, and they would listen to what he said. I can remember looking up to him, thinking he was so cool, and wanting to be like him.

Ricky was one of those kids who had that "golden touch." No matter what he did — be it sports, games, music or activities, he always did great in it, and it came easily for him! He played left

Ricky playing on the Littleton Cougars football team

Ricky with his Kick, Punt and Throw trophies

Debbie acting as Ricky's Cougar cheerleader

defensive end, running back, kicker and punter in football — and he loved playing all those positions. His coach tried to get him to pick one main position, but he would not do it. He had such a desire and thrill for the game, he wanted to do it all. Ricky won the "Kick, Punt and Throw" competitions every year, which were held by the Littleton Football League.

My dad enjoyed taking home movies of Ricky playing football all over the field both offensively and defensively. He played for the Cougars, and their uniforms were black and white. Of course, since I thought he was so great, I wanted to be a cheerleader for his team. I was around four or five years old. All the other little sisters and I got together and started the Cougar cheer squad. We wore these little dresses that were made out of black-and-white fur material that looked like a leopard print. I loved yelling for him and shaking my pom-poms. All of us little girls had no idea what we were doing, but we had a great time yelling and screaming at the top of our lungs. I think Ricky liked it too because every once in awhile he would look my way and give me a big smile.

Ricky also enjoyed playing soccer. I remember Mom telling me a story where Ricky really wanted to play soccer with our brother Charlie. He would go to the games to watch, and he would beg my mom to play. At first my mom did not want him to play because she wanted to keep Charlie and Ricky in different sports so they would not compete against each other (they were only eleven months apart). Now, Charlie's soccer team was not doing too well. They were losing every game that season but for some reason, Ricky still wanted to play. Mom talked to the coach and he allowed Ricky to play on the team. The very first game he played, they won because Ricky was so excited, positive and full of energy running all around the field getting the ball. His enthusiasm rubbed off on his teammates. It was not like Ricky was an experienced soccer player; it was because he had an infectious, positive attitude. Ricky was determined to do his best and play whole-heartedly.

Ricky playing baseball for Littleton Cougars

Rick also liked playing pitcher and shortstop in baseball. He did a great job and struck out a lot of hitters. He liked to be in the center of the field where the action was taking place. It was fun to go to his games and yell for him. Plus, my mom would let us kids get a treat at the game like candy or a popsicle. When he played baseball, I started to notice girls showing up at his games. They would stand over by the side, looking pretty and yelling for him and his teammates. I also

Playing Baseball
L to R: Bruce, Ricky, Charlie

Playing Hockey
L to R: Ricky and Charlie

noticed Ricky would take off his cap and flip his hair a little bit — obviously trying to show off for the girls. At that time, I thought the girls were dumb. I couldn't understand why they would giggle just because he flipped his hair.

Ricky's favorite sport was hockey. He loved being a goalie. He had passion and determination for the sport, and he was not afraid to have all of the hard slap shots hitting him. Coaches noticed his playing skills, and some newspapers wrote articles about his goal tending. I believe some scouts even checked him out for professional hockey. I remember Ricky and my brothers Charlie and Bruce playing hockey in my parent's basement doing slap shots against all the walls, laughing and challenging each other. They would also use the fireplace as their main goal. My poor mom, she had black marks all over the walls. Thank God the walls were made out of cement. If weather permitted, my brothers went outside and played hockey against the garage door. Needless to say, that was full of black marks too, which did not make my dad happy. Not only did Ricky play hockey, but Charlie and Bruce also played hockey. Actually, Charlie was a better player than Ricky or Bruce. He also played a lot longer. Our family lived and breathed hockey for many years. Of course, being the youngest, I was dragged to every hockey game in-state and out-of-state. I was around the age of five when I started hanging out at ice arenas. It was cold — and I didn't like it at first. However, as I got older, I started to realize that my brothers had cute teammates. Then of course, I loved going!

Over the years, my family often traveled to other cities for regional and national hockey tournaments. I didn't mind going because that gave me an opportunity to hang out with all the teenage hockey players. I was probably around eleven or twelve years old and at that age; fifteen and sixteen year old boys were pretty darn cute and exciting.

I also remember at the hockey games, hearing other parents talk about Ricky and Charlie. They would say Charlie was as "fast as lightning" and Ricky was a "stone wall," which was true. Charlie got all the goals. Ricky blocked all the shots. It was fun to watch them play together and both contribute so much to the success of their team. It was also funny hearing my dad screaming above all the other parents, "Get

Ricky played for the Heritage High School hockey team

Ricky played for the Heritage High School hockey team

that goal! Get the puck! Block that goal! Behind you! Check him!" and most importantly, "Blockhead or Idiot!" Of course, that was directed toward the referee. Mom just sat there and observed. She only yelled if another player checked one of her boys. That didn't sit well with her. Then you heard her yell, "Blockhead!" too.

I'm not sure where Ricky got all of his energy to play all of these sports, but I admired it, and I tried to copy it.

I think Ricky's favorite pastimes were fishing, hiking and camping. He loved the mountains as much as I did. They gave

Ricky and Debbie Hiking

Cleaning Fish - One of the many times
he led the family to a high-altitude lake
for some fishing
L to R: Charlie, Debbie, Ricky, Dad

him a sense of serenity. Like everything else he did, he was a good fisherman. He had his rod and reel with him no matter where he went. It seemed like every time he threw in his line, he would catch a fish larger than fourteen inches. It was unbelievable and very annoying. The rest of the family tried fishing, but we didn't catch anything. What also amazed me about Rick was how he always managed to influence or lead my parents and siblings to go on a hike or Jeep trail that would just "happen" to lead to a high-altitude lake, stream or fishing hole. The majority of the time, we did not want to go where Ricky wanted to go, but he seemed to convince us one way or another, and we would end up in a fishing spot. Needless to say, I remember a few times my dad got very angry because Ricky forgot about time — and we were always waiting, waiting and waiting!

Ricky, the audacious spirit, would climb a ridge or mountain just to see what was on the other side. I think it rubbed off on me, because I enjoy doing that too. Whenever we climbed or hiked, Ricky would stop and dig for rocks. No matter where Ricky dug, he was always the first to find the most beautiful quartz crystals, garnets, aquamarines or some other type of cool rock with either gold or silver in it. The rest of us dug for hours, and of course, found nothing. There was never a dull moment with Ricky. Being with him was always a fun adventure.

Ricky was cute in his younger days and the girls always noticed him. One time, my gymnastics team was having an award ceremony for me. My mom made Ricky, Charlie and Bruce go to support me. Of course, they complained all the way over to the gym. They said it would be boring and just girls. To their surprise, they discovered a room full of girls their age. Oh, their little blue eyes and interest perked up when they got in that room full of cute girls.

I recall looking out of the corner of my eye, seeing Ricky

Ricky and Dad - searching for quartz crystals on top of Mt. Antero

Ricky in our backyard during high school

talking and flirting with all these girls. He was trying to be "Mr. Charmer," and of course, Charlie and Bruce were quietly following Ricky's example and started flirting too. I turned away for a moment to talk to my coach and when I looked back, my brothers were all gone! And all the girls too! So my parents and I went outside looking for them in the parking lot, and sure enough, there was Ricky with my brothers having a huge snowball fight with all these girls. I would say it was ten or so girls against those three. They were all giggling and flirting. I thought, *"not again! Now I will have to go to practice tomorrow and listen to all these girls talk about how cute Ricky, Charlie and Bruce are."* Of course, that was

Ricky on his motorcycle

exactly what happened. I was completely annoyed because my brothers got more attention than I did, and of course, I was not surprised to discover that Ricky was the one who persuaded them to go outside.

The one time I was really protective of Ricky was when I was in junior high and he was in high school. I was outside in my parents' backyard, which backs up to my junior high school. Three girls came up to the fence asking me, "Are you Debbie Nau? Do you have two brothers named Ricky and Charlie?"

Of course, I said, "Yes and why?"

They started to rattle off how cute Ricky and Charlie were and that they really liked them. I remember feeling very protective and not wanting these girls to like my brothers. They asked me if I would give them our home phone number so they could call Ricky and Charlie. Well, I gave them a phone number… I just didn't know whose phone number it was. I completely lied to them. I didn't want these girls calling! In my eyes, they were not good enough for Ricky or Charlie.

Ricky definitely had a time when he was very popular, well liked — and I was very proud of him. Unfortunately, late in his junior year and throughout his senior year of high school Ricky faced a turning point in his life. He apparently started to do drugs. I honestly don't know what triggered his desire to want to do drugs — but that became a pivotal point in his story.

Ricky hung out with a neighborhood kid we'll call "Joe Dumb," who I hate to say, did not have much ambition and was a loser in my eyes. I do not know why Ricky wanted to be friends with Joe Dumb. We all felt he was a bad influence. I guess Ricky thought he was cool and popular, when in fact, he wasn't. For some reason, Ricky was drawn to Joe, and he would listen to what he had to say. Ricky once told my brother that he took drugs because Joe commented to him, "If you are a strong person you can handle it." Ricky took that comment as a challenge. He wanted to prove to Joe that he could handle drugs. I don't understand why.

My mom got upset when Ricky hung out with Joe Dumb — she knew that he had a negative impact on him. Every time any of us told Ricky not to hang with him, it just pushed Ricky to be with Joe more. I know in my heart that Joe convinced Ricky to do drugs. It makes me angry just thinking about it.

I was also shocked and dismayed that Ricky started to become a follower and not the leader that he had always been. When he started doing drugs, it changed him physically, mentally and emotionally. I assume it was the influence of pot that changed his personality. I have a feeling that Ricky thought he was invincible; he could do whatever he wanted, and it would not affect him since he always had that "golden touch." But it did.

He started to slack off in sports. His reaction time became slower. He didn't seem interested in camping, hiking or hanging out with our family anymore. All he wanted to do was sit around and listen to music. He quit working out with weights and he started to loose weight. He looked messy and he appeared to be emotionally withdrawn. I had a difficult time accepting that someone with such a zest and enthusiasm for life would transform into someone with no real life. I became sad for him, as I literally watched his light burn out.

Both of my brothers, Charlie and Ricky, graduated from Heritage High School in June 1980. Looking back on pictures, Charlie was dressed in a suit, excited and smiling; Ricky was in jeans and a t-shirt, and he didn't seem to care. I guess that is what happens when negative people and substances affect your personality.

After graduation, I think Ricky felt lost and not sure what to do. He did not have any friends anymore. They were all leaving for college or didn't want to hang out with him since he'd developed a reputation for doing drugs. Ricky didn't have the desire to go to college. Studying was not his strong suit. So, Ricky decided to join the Navy to see what opportunities awaited him. I thought it was a great decision! It would get him away from the people who, I believed in my heart, were destroying him — not only his wonderful personality, but also his ambition and desire for life.

Class of 1980
Ricky and Charlie

Ricky left for the Navy soon after graduation. He was so excited, and a flicker of light was burning bright again. I was happy for him, but I was really going to miss him. It made me sad to think our times of hanging out together were over. Ricky, Charlie, Bruce and I (the four younger kids) were all very close as kids and did everything together. We were all buddies who shared lots of fun memories and supported each other

Ricky leaving for the Navy

through sports, school and family issues. We wouldn't even open up Christmas presents without each other.

To see Rick start a whole new adventure without us was sad but exciting, and it was something we understood he desperately needed. He had always been an outgoing person. He needed to see things, do things, and experience life. He was full of adventure, vibrant and enthusiastic — and he loved living.

Little did I know I would never see him this way again.

CHAPTER THREE

Life Never Turns Out
the Way You Think

It was a warm, sunny Colorado fall day in October of 1981 and autumn was in the air. The days were warm and the evenings were chilly. The leaves were turning yellow, orange and red and everything was beautiful! The family was doing really well. My brother Jim was living in Seattle and working at a bank. My brother Gene was finishing up his Masters of Science degree in Tennessee. My sister Theresa was happily married and living in Littleton. Jeff was working on helicopters in Louisiana. Charlie was attending technical school in Denver. Bruce was working construction in Littleton, and Ricky was serving on the *USS Blue Ridge* a command ship in Japan. I was fifteen years old and had started my sophomore year at Heritage High School. I was excited, meeting new friends, checking out boys, and looking forward to a whole bunch of new experiences. For once, I was starting to feel a little bit like an adult. There were parties to go to and football games to attend. Life was good, and I was happy!

Then one day in October, my mom and dad started to receive very odd and weird letters from my brother Ricky. He wrote with a thick, black marker in large letters expressing very strange ideas.

It was confusing reading his letters, and we didn't understand what was going on. Ricky kept writing about the world not being balanced and that there were evil spirits. He stated that the devil was taking over the world, and there was a major war between good and evil. The letters were not written in comprehensible sentences. It was just one weird thought after another. My family and I were upset and did not know what to think about the situation or what was happening with Ricky. I was starting to wonder if Ricky was partying in Japan and doing drugs. I just couldn't figure out why he would write such weird letters. I just prayed to God that he was okay.

It was now November and my parents were very concerned. They had not heard anything from Ricky for quite awhile. My mom contacted the Navy chaplain and went down to the office to talk to him. They sent a telegram through the Red Cross to the USS *Blue Ridge*, asking about Ricky's status. All the *Blue Ridge* sent back was that Ricky was gone. He was honorably discharged. What? We were in shock and disbelief! Why would they release him? What in the world was going on? The lack of knowledge of what happened to Ricky and why he was released was very frustrating. My parents could not get any answers from anyone, and we had no idea where he was.

A few weeks later, on the Sunday before Thanksgiving of '81, my mom got a phone call from Ricky.

"Mom, I'm at the bus station in downtown Denver. Can you come get me?" asked Ricky with a strange urgency.

"I will be right there," she said right away like any concerned mother.

My mom left immediately and drove downtown to pick Ricky up. When she saw him at the station, she was completely stunned by his gaunt appearance. She helped move his bags to the car, and they got in. At first, they sat together in silence — Mom driving, uncertain as to what she should say. Finally, she spoke up and said, "Ricky, you could have come home anytime."

Ricky was acting strange and responded in an almost matter-of-fact tone. "I couldn't," he said, "the demons have followed me from Japan, and I didn't want to bring them home. I am afraid they are following us now."

Mom was very upset and scared for him because her child looked so sick, and she didn't understand what he was saying or why he was saying these things. She reassured him, "It's okay. I'm taking you home to get some food and rest and everything will be better tomorrow."

When Ricky walked in the front door, I was shocked and stunned by his appearance. He looked completely exhausted and distraught. He didn't look like the brother I knew and loved but looked like a different person. He was dirty and smelly as though he was sleeping on the streets. He was very thin; I could see his shoulder bones protruding out of his shirt. His skin was very pale with a whitish blue color and he had dark back circles under his eyes. I didn't know what to say or what to do. I felt nervous and scared. At first, Ricky didn't say anything or even looked at us; he just looked at the floor. You could tell he was very exhausted because of his slumping shoulders and heading hanging down.

After a while, he would just stare at us. Each sibling asked him questions like: "Are you okay? Do you want some food? Do you want a blanket? What can we do to help?"

He would just nod "yes." You could tell something was terribly wrong. He was very scared, and he wouldn't let go of his crucifix, rosary and prayer book. He was too afraid to go into his bedroom downstairs. He would only lay down on the floor in the living room next to the fireplace and go in and out of trance-like states. He would occasionally mention bizarre ideas about God and demons.

"The God from Japan is going to come destroy the God here," he said emphatically. "The demons from Japan are evil. They're going to destroy the world." He would go back and forth in his comments about demons and aliens from outer space. "The aliens are working against God, they will destroy you."

My brothers Charlie and Bruce and I were so deeply sad because we were utterly helpless. He was so terrified it was heartbreaking to watch. I kept reassuring him, "It's okay Rick, we will protect you. Nothing is going to hurt you. Just get some rest. You look so very tired. Close your eyes, it's okay."

He didn't want to be alone, so my brothers and I offered to stay up with him. Bruce lay on one side of him on the floor, I lay on the other side, and Charlie was on the couch. We gathered blankets around Ricky's body so he would feel protected. We kept the fire going and stayed with him all night long.

He dozed off for a little while and then he would wake up in panic shouting, "They're after me!" he cried. "The demons are outside!"

Bruce and I would gently pat the side of his arm and comfort him by saying, "It's okay." I would continuously say this until he would settle down. While I was lying there on the floor looking at Ricky, I remember tears flooding my eyes wondering what happened to my brother and feeling so sorry for him. I whispered in his ear while he was sleeping, "I'm so sorry."

I felt tremendous guilt for thinking negative thoughts about him, and that he was doing drugs in Japan. That was definitely not the case! This situation was something different and something very serious. He wasn't the brother I remembered, and I saw no light burning within him. I had a weird feeling at that time that Ricky coming home was going to change our lives forever. I just didn't realize how much.

During the next few days, we all started to realize that Ricky definitely had some type of mental illness. Ricky kept grabbing his stomach and would hold himself tightly with tears in his eyes because he felt such deep pain. He thought his insides were falling out. Ricky grabbed his eyes and cried, "The demons are coming out of my eyes! Please help me!"

My mom and dad were dumbfounded and didn't know what to say. Mom asked, "What do you mean, Rick? What's wrong with your eyes?"

Ricky said, "God is in my right eye and Satan is in my left eye."

Dad asked, "How is God in your right eye?"

Ricky started yelling, "The light is in my right and the dark is in my left! It hurts!"

My mom grabbed a cold cloth to put on his eyes. It did calm Ricky down a little bit. Ricky had some type of war going on in his mind between good and evil. Ricky thought monsters were invading his mind. Plus, he was hearing some type of evil voice because he would stare at the wall or ceiling, and then he would answer as though someone was speaking to him. It was quite chilling to watch. To see my brother display signs of mental illness was very scary, confusing and upsetting. I wanted to help but I had no idea how. I wanted to hug him and tell him everything would be okay, but Ricky would not allow anyone to touch him because it was physically painful for him.

Ricky would not leave the house, and hardly ate those first few days. My dad was extremely upset and concerned, so he thought it would be good to get Ricky outside for some fresh air. My dad took him for a walk up the street. However, they didn't get very far because the sun was very painful to Ricky's eyes. It was excruciating for him. He was scared, and he couldn't see where he was walking. Starting to panic he got very upset to the point of crying. He kept saying to my dad, "Please take me home! The sun is hurting my eyes! I'm in pain!"

My dad said, "It's okay, Rick. Your eyes will adjust to the light."

"No! My eyes hurt, they are burning" Ricky cried. "I can't see! I want to go home now!"

Dad was getting scared and confused, he told Ricky, "Okay, okay, it's all right. Let's turn around and go back home."

My father held his arm tightly and helped him slowly walk back to the house while comforting his fears. Dad spoke to him in a calming voice, "It's okay, Rick. It's okay. I'm taking you home. Just hold onto my arm. We are almost there."

A few days later, Ricky told my parents, "A couple of women at a bar in Japan put an evil curse on me, and that is why I am sick."

He believed in his heart that these women did this because his friend told the women to take a hike when they weren't interested in hooking up with them. Ricky told my parents, "One of the women was pointing her finger at me saying weird things. I felt a sharp pain in my head. I know that's when it happened! The evil spirits were all around me." He looked so certain. "They have been following me ever since. I can't get away from them," he declared, completely committed to the story.

My parents knew Ricky desperately needed to see a doctor. For days, they kept trying to get Ricky to go to the hospital but he would not go. I know it was because he was terrified to leave the house in fear of the demons. After much persuasion, they finally got Ricky to agree to go see a doctor at the Veterans Hospital in Denver. Even when they arrived at the hospital, they sat in the car and persuaded Ricky for over an hour to get him to go into the building.

My mom comforted him and said, "It's okay, Rick. They can help you."

Of course, Ricky would not listen.

My dad was more stern and said, "The doctors can help you. We won't leave you. You need to go in."

Finally, Ricky relented and agreed to go in.

At the Veterans Hospital, Ricky was very impatient and kept making weird and bizarre comments. It took hours of waiting to get Ricky through the paperwork and process of admitting him to the hospital. Once he was admitted, my parents spoke with a young doctor and explained all of Ricky's symptoms, such as, paranoia, physical pain, hallucinations and delusions. The doctor also observed and spoke to Ricky. He seemed to understand Ricky's situation immediately.

He told my parents, "I'm sorry, but Ricky has schizophrenia."

I could only imagine what my parents felt and thought! My dad was deeply heartbroken because he has schizophrenia in his family history. Ricky must have been carrying the predisposition gene to inherit this terrible disease, which can be triggered by drugs. Schizophrenia is a neurological brain disease that interferes with a person's ability to think clearly, manage emotions, make decisions, and relate to others. Some specific abnormalities are delusions, hallucinations, perception of hearing internal voices, and experience of physical sensations.

I could see the agony in my parent's eyes to now know their son was mentally ill, and he would probably never be normal again. Unfortunately, the doctor had told my parents, "There is no cure for schizophrenia, only medications to try to normalize the behaviors."

They had a lot of questions. What do we do? How do we handle it? We all had to stay positive and get Ricky the help that he needed.

Ricky was admitted and stayed at the Veterans Hospital for two months. The doctors tried different medications to help him.

Unfortunately, most of the medications gave him bad side effects or made him feel like a zombie. My parents would go visit Ricky at the hospital, but he was usually drugged out, which shortened the visits. Occasionally, they would let Ricky come home for the weekend. At this time, none of us minded. We were all happy to see him and had high hopes that he would get the help that he needed; however, Ricky was very distant and the conversations were short due to the medication. At least he was home and had a little family interaction. No words were said, but I think we all felt emptiness, as we knew Ricky would never be the same, nor would the family dynamic. It was like Ricky had left us.

Personally, I had a hard time adjusting to the idea that Ricky was sick. I wanted to go visit him in the hospital but I couldn't. I just didn't have the heart to see him in a facility with other sick people. It was painful and confusing for me to see my handsome, smart and active brother — and someone I loved and adored — transformed into a non-person I couldn't understand or comprehend. He became so empty, distant and cold. He had so much potential, and I didn't understand why he had to get sick. None of this made sense to me.

My birthday is a week before Christmas, and it happened to fall on Friday that year. Ricky came home to visit that weekend. It was to be my sweet sixteenth birthday. I tried to be excited about it, but it was hard when my mind was on Ricky and I was worried about how the weekend would go. That day, my high school basketball team was playing a game against another Littleton high school called Arapahoe High School. Most of my close friends from junior high school went to Arapahoe. I was really excited to go to the game, celebrate my birthday, and see my old friends and my old boyfriend. At least for a couple of hours, I was able to enjoy myself and get my mind off Ricky. As time went on, moments like these became valuable to me, as I soon realized I desperately needed them. Needless to say, those happy few hours quickly faded when I returned home to see and deal with the emotional aspects of Ricky and his illness.

Ricky came home for Christmas Eve and Christmas Day. It was not the fun, joyful Christmas that we usually experienced. Ricky got upset when we arrived at the church parking lot for Christmas Midnight Mass. He became very nervous and started tapping his hand on his knee. From the reflection of the parking lot light, I could see a little sweat on his forehead. Ricky was becoming anxious, and he didn't want to go inside because he said, "It's dark, the parking lot is too dark! There are too many people," he declared. "I'm scared to walk over there."

As we sat in the car, my mom gently touched Ricky's arm and said, "You don't have to be afraid. You're protected in church."

Ricky just stared at her.

She then said, "It's okay, we will walk beside you."

"Don't worry Rick, no one will hurt you." I kept agreeing with my mom and repeated what she said to try to persuade Ricky into getting out of the car.

At first, he didn't acknowledge us for a few minutes and then he stated again, his voice trembling, "I'm scared!"

My mom looked at him lovingly and said in a very calm, sweet voice, "We will both walk on each side of you, you will be okay."

I jumped in to help Mom and said, "We will protect you, Rick."

He nodded his head "yes" and only agreed to go into the church if we sat in the very last row.

As we walked in, Mom was on one side; I was on the other. Ricky kept his head down and didn't look at anyone. We sat in the very last row by the corner. Ricky sat quietly through most of the mass, but you could see he was starting to get very nervous because his leg started to shake and he squeezed his hands into fists.

My mom realized immediately that she had to get Ricky out of church a few minutes early. She looked at me and nodded her head to the side as to tell me, "Let's go!"

By the almost frantic look of her eyes, I knew that meant *now!* My mom touched Ricky's leg and patted it to say to him, "Let's go." Ricky understood.

We all quietly got up and went out the side door. Mom was afraid Ricky would get upset with all the people walking too close to him. She did not want him to make any weird comments about the devil or demons since we were at church. People would not understand and would probably freak out or get upset. It was a good thing my mom noticed his reactions because as soon as we got back to the car, Ricky became very distraught.

He kept mumbling nonstop in a frustrated voice: "The evil spirits are coming! They're coming from Japan! They are going destroy our church and us!"

My mom tried to calm Ricky down all the way home. She kept interrupting him with counter-comments such as, "Rick, the demons are not coming; it's part of your illness. You have to trust me that you're going to be okay. The church will be okay. We're almost home."

I quietly sat in the backseat and prayed all the way home for God to help and heal Ricky.

The next day, Christmas dinner wasn't much fun either. It was actually very quiet, which is odd for ten people sitting at the table. Everyone was cautious as to what to say because no one wanted to upset or trigger any reactions from Ricky. We had no idea what he was thinking or seeing; we knew his thoughts were not in a normal place. We just quietly ate our food and then watched football in a subdued manner.

A few days later, my brother Jeff got married. Ricky was very withdrawn at the wedding and kept to himself. He really did not want to participate in the wedding because it was hard for him to be around people. The social noise bothered him. I remember at the reception, I stood at the top of the staircase with my brother Charlie by my side. As I looked down to watch the party activities, I noticed Ricky standing in the corner where it was a little bit dark. He looked very scared and a little shaken. He had his arms crossed in front of him, like he was squeezing himself. I knew he was hearing voices by his facial expressions. He kept squeezing his eyes shut and then opening them up really wide to stare. Also he kept moving his mouth from side to side like he was talking weird. A deep sorrow filled my heart.

I told Charlie, "Look at Ricky, he is so upset. He's hiding in the corner. I'm going to go tell Mom." Charlie nodded in agreement. So I went to my mom and dad to let them know about Ricky — and that I thought he really needed to leave. It was just too much for him. My parents agreed and left immediately.

The last few months had been hard. Christmas break came to an end and the first semester of high school was almost over. I went from extreme feelings of excitement about starting high school to the sadness of dealing with my brother in his illness and watching his suffering. Of course, I didn't have anyone to talk to. My peers were only sixteen years old. My friends were only interested in parties and boys, so what advice could they possibly give me?

So I decided to hold it all in

Watching Ricky at Jeff's wedding reception
L to R: Debbie and Charlie

and not tell anyone. It was better to act fake and happy than to share with everyone that I had a mentally ill brother. Plus, I was a little embarrassed. Of course, I felt guilty for feeling embarrassed, and it turned into a vicious cycle of emotions — embarrassment, guilt, embarrassment, guilt, and round and round. Damn, what a way to start high school! I had just turned sixteen! I should be having fun, meeting boys, and going on my first date! Unfortunately, my mind and concerns were only on Ricky.

CHAPTER FOUR

Finding Balance in My Unbalanced World

It was now January 1982, and Ricky was released from the Veterans Hospital. The hospital felt he was doing well enough that he could come home. Unfortunately, after Ricky got home he quit taking his medication. He felt that the medication made him worse, and he couldn't handle the bad side effects. My mom tried to do everything she could to get him to take his medication.

"Please Ricky, take your medicine," Mom pleaded.

"No!" he argued. "It makes me sick!"

Mom's eyes darted and her voice quivered from the frustration. "Please Rick, I will make your favorite dinner if you take just one pill."

"No!" he screamed.

She tried to manipulate him by putting his medication in his orange juice or mixing it up in his food. She even resorted to bribing him with treats or money. Nothing worked. We all knew he needed it, but for schizophrenics, they do not have any comprehension of necessity. Ricky honestly believed he was not sick and did not need medication.

Without medication, Ricky's illness started to worsen. His

hallucinations increased, and he saw demons, monsters and insects. He heard more voices. Frantically he said, "They're telling me not to take the medication." He stood in the corner and covered the left side of his head and ear with his hand, so he would not hear the demons. Sometimes you could hear him say, "Leave me alone. I believe in God, go away! No! I don't believe you."

He also experienced bad headaches and terrible migraines. Ricky often welled up in tears because the pain would be excruciating. We all felt his anguish. The physical pain he kept experiencing must have been terrible. He was terribly disturbed. No matter what, we just could not get him to realize that this was part of his illness, and he needed to take his medication. We would all try to encourage him to take his medication. "Please Rick, the medication might help your head pains. Ricky, you won't know if the medication works until you try it. Please Rick, you're ill. You need medication!" we each begged in sadness.

The nights were becoming more stressful. It was tough to sleep and I fought with my pillows. The night just wouldn't let go. The battle over medications was starting to wear on family. How do you get a mentally ill person to think a rational thought? It was impossible and we needed help.

My oldest brother Jim lived in Seattle. A very loving, gentle and caring man who didn't hesitate to jump in and try to help his little brother, which I admired. Jim talked my parents into letting Ricky go to Seattle to stay with him for a month. Jim wanted to take Ricky to a specialist to see if he or she could help him. I think deep in our hearts we were all hoping for a small miracle, that Jim would be able help Ricky.

I believe Ricky was also happy to go see Jim in Seattle. Ricky always got along great with Jim, and they had a close relationship. Even as kids, Jim hung out with Ricky. Occasionally, he allowed

Ricky to tag along with him and his friends, even though they were young teenagers and Ricky was a little boy. Ricky enjoyed being with them every moment that he could. He thought they were extremely cool. Actually, Jim and Ricky looked and acted a lot alike. Their mannerisms were the same; they had the same smile and tone of voice. When they were together, you definitely knew they were brothers — there was a special bond between them. Without really understanding his type of mental illness Jim thought that their friendship and bond as brothers would make the difference.

While Ricky was in Seattle, Jim took him to a specialist who studied chemical imbalances of the brain through natural techniques. I don't remember what doctor or facility Jim went to, but I do know they did a CAT scan, hair analysis, blood work and detailed studies of Ricky's diet. From the CAT scan, the doctors found that Ricky had a bruise on his brain, probably from playing football, but no one knows for sure. We are not positive if that contributed to Ricky getting schizophrenia, but it could have been a possible factor, along with him trying drugs in high school. The hair analysis also found that Ricky had too much copper in his body, which I guess is common amongst schizophrenics. The doctors stated that Ricky was hypoglycemic too. They suggested a certain type of diet, vitamins and health foods to try to rebalance the chemicals in his brain.

I think for a few weeks, Ricky cooperated with Jim. He tried the diet and ate all the foods that the doctor suggested. Jim cooked each of his meals to make sure he ate correctly. Jim felt that the diet worked somewhat well. Ricky seemed better for a short time; he talked with a clear voice, he had no physical pains, and he did not seem paranoid. However, occasionally he would still hear voices and stare into space.

Jim could hear Ricky in his bedroom saying, "No, I can't do that. You don't know what you're talking about. I don't want to listen to you! Go away!"

There were times when Jim and Ricky were watching television, and Jim noticed Ricky was either staring at the wall or watching "something" on the wall. He definitely was not paying attention to the television.

One particular day, Jim became very concerned. He caught Ricky walking up and down the sidewalk in his neighborhood, acting very weird. Ricky kept mumbling words to himself, "I can't hear you! Yes, I can do that! No, I can't do that." Ricky also yelled at the sky, "I know the gods are coming! Go away, you're bothering me!" Ricky then swiped his arms in all different directions as if he was swiping things out of thin air. "Get out of my way!" he yelled.

Jim ran outside in fear of the neighbors calling the police. He gently spoke to Ricky and said, "Ricky, why don't you come in? They will leave you alone if you come inside of the house."

Ricky just stood and stared in amazement because Jim understood what was happening to him. Ricky did not hesitate to follow Jim back into the house. I think at that moment, Jim knew that Ricky's illness was way more serious and difficult than what he'd imagined. He knew it was going to be a long road.

In the middle of February, Ricky came home from Seattle. Jim had to go back to work. He was worried about leaving Ricky home alone all day. Plus, Ricky was starting to get bored and wanted to come home. At first, he did pretty well. He seemed to be feeling okay. He was still trying to eat the healthy foods that Jim and the doctor had suggested.

With Ricky feeling and doing a little bit better, he decided to go buy a car without anyone knowing. He had some money that he earned from the Navy. My parents were frustrated when he showed up with a car because they felt he was not in a best position to be driving and taking care of a car. Ricky explained that he wanted to go to the movies or grocery story by himself. My parents understand Ricky's thought process but they still tried to encourage him to take the car back or sell it. Of course, Ricky just ignored them.

Ricky improvement only lasted a couple of weeks. He stopped following his diet because he believed it was not working anymore. After that we noticed a sharp decline in his mental state. He started to become a lot more withdrawn and very depressed. He did not have any desire for life.

Based on the scared look on his face, and the way his eyes darted at each one of us, I believe he was starting to see more monsters, aliens and demons. Ricky always looked around our heads and around our backs, as if he was seeing something hiding behind us or coming out of our bodies. He also poked us to see if we were real. He started to hear voices more frequently, because he was talking to the wall, ceiling or into midair more often. I believe the voices were telling him to kill himself, because he often said, "They told me I'm not going to be here much longer. It's better on the other side. I don't want to live with the demons anymore."

My brothers and I both similarly responded, "Don't listen to the voices, Rick. They are wrong. It's part of your illness."

I could tell by watching his behavior that he was drastically changing. We were all starting to become very concerned.

My parents took Ricky to a few different doctors over the next couple of weeks. I can't remember all of them or where they were located. My parents didn't get much help. One doctor validated that Ricky had schizophrenia but would not give him any medication. My parents called other doctors, and they only suggested we take Ricky to another doctor or facility. So my parents called them and received no help. My parents tried Rose Medical Hospital for help but their facilities were all full. They felt disappointed because they didn't get any response or necessary help.

In March 1982, I came home from school to an empty, quiet house. I thought it was odd because Ricky always hung around upstairs because of his fears of the demons living downstairs. He always thought the demons came to find him in his bedroom. I decided to go downstairs to see if Ricky was okay. When I got to the bottom of the stairs, I saw Ricky sitting on the couch with a string tied extremely tight around his neck. He was so pale and barely breathing. The string was cutting off his circulation.

I was scared to death! I rushed over to him and cried, "Ricky! What are you doing?" I asked in horror as my shaking fingers tried to loosen the grip of the string.

Ricky looked at me with such a vacant expression. He didn't answer but just stared into space, and then said, "I want to die," in a weak, dispassionate voice, that can only be described as pitiful.

I was stunned! Now I was shaking and tormented. I didn't know what to do so I rushed upstairs to the phone and called my mom. "Mom!" I shrieked into the phone as I cried, "Ricky is trying to kill himself."

Silence followed and then she said, "Okay, I will be right home!"

As she rushed home from work, I went back downstairs to try to help Ricky. He would not let me help him. He kept pushing my hands away. I started to cry out of fear and frustration, "Ricky, stop! Let me help you!"

He became weak, so I was able to move his hands out of the way. I tried to loosen the string, but I was having a very difficult time because I could not stop shaking! "Damn it! I can't get it loose! Mom will be home in a minute," I cried.

I didn't know what to do, so I ran upstairs to pace the floor as I waited for my mom to get home. She got home within a few minutes. She rushed downstairs to find Ricky now in his bedroom lying on his bed, as if he was waiting to die. Mom cautiously sat next to Ricky on the bed, and then she lovingly stroked his hair and said, "I see you got yourself into a difficult situation. Everything is going to be fine."

Ricky didn't respond. He just stared at her with emptiness.

She managed to stay patient and calmly spoke to him as she worked at untying the string. "It's okay, Rick, I'm going to get this untied. I'm not sure why you did this, but I want you around. Don't be afraid. Everything is going to be fine." Thank goodness she kept her cool. She talked to Ricky with such a quiet, soothing voice.

As I stood watching by the bedroom door, hearing her voice calmed my anxiety, too. My mom stayed focused and got the string untied quickly. I still don't know how she did it because the string was so tight. Ricky's neck was bright red with a bruise all around it. After a few minutes, the color slowly returned to his face.

Mom gently patted Ricky on the stomach and said, "Please don't do that again." Mom then made Ricky go upstairs and lay down on the couch so she could keep an eye on him. It was a scary situation for me because looking deep into Ricky's blue eyes, I could not let go of the feeling of seeing such deep sadness within his soul. It wrenched my very heart and soul.

Immediately after this incident, my mom searched the yellow pages of the phone book and found a psychiatrist at Rocky Mountain Hospital. The next morning, my mom called and got an appointment for that day. My parents quickly took Ricky over to the hospital. After speaking to the doctor and giving him a detailed description of Ricky's behavior, the doctor knew Ricky desperately needed help. The only way the doctor could get him committed into the hospital was to say he was an alcoholic because they had no openings for mental illness. The hospital had just opened a new ward for alcoholics, and Ricky was the first patient.

During their meeting, the doctor said, "Mr. and Mrs. Nau, Ricky may have inherited schizophrenia. This disease usually comes forth in males around the age of eighteen," he said. "If you carry the gene for schizophrenia, this illness could be triggered by extreme stress (for instance, joining the military) or taking any type of drugs."

Like most parents when they hear their child inherited an illness, felt shocked and broken hearted. They were in disbelief that their son inherited this horrible disease and probably brought it out by taking drugs. Until that day, my parents really had no knowledge about schizophrenia, and it had never occurred to them that it was an inheritable disease. There had been some schizophrenia on my dad's side of the family but they did not know much about the illness. Knowing Ricky's situation, the doctor promptly got Ricky on medication called Haldal.

During this time, I started spring break at school. I didn't go anywhere or see anyone. I felt frustrated and angry that I had no ability to help Ricky. I also had no one to talk to. I started to realize I wasn't fitting into school, and I wasn't making any new friends. I guess I really didn't care by this time. I was feeling depressed, and I was missing my old friends who had gone to another high school. At this moment, I knew I needed to change schools and get back with the friends I enjoyed being around. I almost felt that it was the only way to keep my sanity.

As soon as I got back to school, I went to the office and filled out the paperwork to be transferred to Arapahoe High School starting my junior year. I felt excited about this decision — and I knew it was the right thing to do. I needed to be around friends who I felt comfortable with and felt I could trust. I even started contacting some of my friends and tried to see them on the weekends. Occasionally, a few of my close guy friends; Brain, Scott and Joe, would come pick me up at my school for lunch. They encouraged me to switch schools. It was just what I needed and wanted to hear! It helped me feel better about myself.

In the middle of April 1982, Rocky Mountain Hospital released Ricky. My parents' insurance only covered thirty days. Since the insurance was up, they had to release him. At this time, my brother Charlie had a regional hockey tournament in Salt Lake City, Utah. My parents could not leave Ricky home alone with Bruce and me. They were afraid that Ricky would either try suicide again, or he would stop taking his medicine and start fights with us. They asked the hospital if there was any way it could keep Ricky one more week while they went to Salt Lake City. Unfortunately, the hospital said no. The only thing the doctor could do was to give my parents a prescription for the medication so they could continue to give it to Ricky on their own. Ricky was still very depressed and could not be left unattended. My parents knew their only option was to take Ricky with them to Salt Lake City so they could keep a close eye on him.

While my parents and Ricky were in Salt Lake City, Ricky acted very disconnected. He would not respond in words if my parents asked him a question, such as, "Rick, do you need anything?"

He would just nod or shake his head.

Whenever my parents walked from the ice arena to the hotel or to the restaurant, Ricky always followed eight feet behind. He would never walk too close to them.

"Come on Rick, you need to stay closer," said Dad. "You can't walk that far behind us."

Ricky just nodded "yes" and moved a couple of feet closer. If people sat close to Ricky at the hockey game, he pumped his knees, he crossed his arms in front of his body, and his eyes widen with fear, as if he afraid they were going to hurt him. He stared people down, giving them the look that said: "Don't you get close to me!"

His hands and legs would twitch in a constant movement like he was about take off for a sprint. "Ricky, why don't you sit at the top of the bleachers so you have more room?" suggested Mom when she saw him twitch.

Once again, he nodded, "yes" and moved to the top of the bleachers to sit by himself.

Ricky also acted claustrophobic. He would not let my parents sit in a booth at a restaurant because he felt closed in. If Ricky did say anything it was, "You're too close," or, "Get away!" He would not allow anyone to stand or sit closer than two or three feet from him.

"Ricky, you have to sit closer to us; we are in a restaurant," Mom quietly pleaded.

"We need to give the waiters their room. Come closer. Don't worry, I'm not going to invade your space."

Ricky just nodded "yes" but would not move.

There were times when Ricky would cross the street without looking for cars or try to walk through a door when it was an automatic exit out. He acted like he was in another world. He walked around empty - he saw and heard nothing.

Mom noticed he was hearing voices because he kept looking up above his head or to the side. She could see him mumbling as if someone was sitting right next to him. She could faintly hear him say, "I can't do that. No, you're wrong. He's not an alien."

She looked at him with a concerned smile to let him know she was aware. My mom always kept a very close eye on him like an eagle watching her eaglets. She never let Ricky walk into a room or area without her. He was never left alone.

Both of my parents were also very concerned with Ricky's physical decline. He showed extreme signs of exhaustion, walked very slowly and breathed heavily. He had become rail thin because he could hardly eat. He looked hollow, pale and empty. There were always dark circles under his eyes. My parents didn't know what to do but to keep him close. They still had another son they needed to take care of and pay attention to. I believe the medication that Ricky was taking at the time basically kept him stoned. He acted like he was in a trance and didn't know where he was. My parents didn't realize it at the time but he was being overdosed on Haldal. The medication was way too strong and gave him bad side effects, such as loss of appetite, jitters, headaches and lack of thought.

Luckily, nothing bad happened while my parents were in Salt Lake City. They were able to enjoy Charlie's hockey games while still doing a good job of being patient and taking care of Ricky.

It was now May of 1982. They were starting cheerleading tryouts at Arapahoe High School. I was excited to try out and get back together with my old friends. It wasn't that I was overly excited about being a cheerleader; I was just excited to be around a group of people and have the opportunity to meet new friends, since I had felt alone all year. I wanted to find some balance in my unbalanced world. I made the varsity squad, and I felt like I had something to look forward to. My home life was stressful and sad. I needed something to focus on besides Ricky — and cheerleading filled that role.

End of school and summertime came quickly. It was June, the sun was shining and I was finally out of school. I was excited because it was now time to start our annual summer league softball team. I was on a team that had started back when I was in sixth grade. We were all good softball players, and we won the championship every year. The girls on the team went to three different high schools.

We always had a blast, because it was fun to see each other again, and we all got along extremely well. I was also starting summer cheerleading practices. I felt at the time that there was hope and things were going to be better. I was around my old friends again, and I was also making new friends. Life was starting to look up, at least for awhile.

Well… the "at least for a little while" only lasted about two weeks. Ricky continued on a downward spiral. It was so heartbreaking to be around him. It is hard to explain how he transformed into another person. His hallucinations were becoming worse. Voices kept telling him to kill himself. He kept talking about the battle of good and evil — and how it was putting pressure on his brain. Paranoia gripped him, and he was scared to go outside. Everyone was after him. He also started developing night terrors. Scared to go to sleep because of monsters, aliens and demons came to his bed at night to attack him and take away his soul.

The lack of eating and sleeping was physically destroying him. I also think the stress was physically taking a toll on my family, too. It was a continuing battle to get Ricky to take medication and to get medication from doctors. I know that personally, I didn't have much of an appetite and was tired all of the time. Trying to fake being happy wasn't easy.

In June, my parents got Ricky into Mount Airy Hospital. The doctor at the hospital informed them that Ricky was being overdosed on his medication Haldal. The doctor immediately switched his medication to Loxitane. The doctor who I'm going to name "Dr. Blockhead" didn't do much for Ricky. He would not even admit to my parents that Ricky had schizophrenia.

My folks participated in a counseling session and told Dr. Blockhead everything that was going on, but he didn't seem too interested to help. They tried to get answers and assistance, but talking to Dr. Blockhead was like talking to a wall. Half of the time, he didn't answer Mom's phone calls. I believe he did not make much of an effort to work with my brother. Ricky told us he never saw or talked to him. Shocking! All things considered. He was a psychiatrist, I thought that was his job, but I guess not.

Ricky was only at Mount Airy Hospital for a few weeks. He didn't get the help that he needed. So, he came home, of course, without any medication because Dr. Blockhead would not give a prescription to my parents. The first day Ricky was home, he was angry and irritable. He walked around the house, yelling in a deranged manner, "Why are you looking at me? Stop staring at me! Stop sending me your evil thoughts!"

No one looked at him. We all tried to avoid him if he walked into the room. Mom pleaded, "Ah Rick, stop it. No one is looking at you." She then demanded, "Go outside and calm down."

Ricky yelled back, "No! They're staring at me! They're making me mad!"

As I was sitting in the living room, I heard Ricky scream at Bruce, "Stop looking at me!" Within a second, Ricky ran up to Bruce and punched him hard in the stomach. Bruce yelled in pain as he bent over to grab his stomach. Ricky had knocked the wind out of him.

Bruce yelled back, "Get away from me!" but Bruce knew not to physically react back. He realized it wasn't Ricky who had hit him but his sickness.

I jumped up and stood next to Bruce. Ricky stood there with his shoulders back with a scowled look on his face. I whispered to Bruce, "You need to leave."

Bruce immediately backed up and left the room. Meanwhile, Mom ran into the room and yelled at Ricky, "You will never hit another sibling again if you are going to stay in this house! Go downstairs!"

Ricky acted outraged because Mom yelled at him. He stomped his feet and went into the backyard. He nervously paced around, yelling and pointing at the sky, "They're looking at me weird. Make them stop!"

I just gave Mom a scared look. She assured, "Don't worry. He will calm down. Just leave him alone and stay away from him."

I went to go see Bruce in his bedroom. "Are you okay?"

By the look on his face, I knew he was deeply hurt and frustrated. In a shaky, low voice he said, "Get out of my room. I want to be alone."

As I closed the door, I turned and said, "I'm glad you didn't hit him back. I'm sorry he hit you." He did not respond. Feeling sorry for him I left.

Later that night, Ricky still acted angry and grumbled, "Your spirits are bothering me! I hate your spirits! Your spirits are going to crucify me!"

"Sorry, Rick, I'm not making them do anything," I said, my voice shaky. I sensed he was getting frustrated with me because he didn't think I was helping him. I went to my bedroom and locked the door.

Within a few minutes, I heard: Pound! Pound! Pound! Ricky banged on my bedroom door. He yelled, "Stop your spirits now`! Leave me alone!"

Frightened and trembling, I did not respond. Then I heard Ricky go outside to the backyard. He came to my bedroom window and started hitting it while he was screaming, "Your spirits are bugging me! Tell them to stop. They are taking over my brain!"

I did not answer. I just sat on my bed with my hands over my ears; afraid he would break the window.

"Stop breathing on me! You're sending me evil spirits!" he

continued to yell angrily.

I didn't know what to think or do. I finally got up and closed my curtains. I just tried to ignore him, but his anger scared me. I was just hoping that the neighbors did not see or hear him. Eventually, my mom realized what was happening and ran outside. In a desperate voice she tried to calm Ricky down. "Ricky, it's okay. Debbie isn't sending you evil spirits, that's part of your illness. Why don't you come with me into the kitchen — they will stop if you come with me. Come on Rick, it's going to be okay."

Eventually, Ricky listened to my mom and left me alone. He went into the kitchen where Mom distracted him and made him help her dry the dishes. I think she started to realize if she got Ricky to think about something else, he would lose his thought process and usually calm down. This was the first time Ricky had showed physical signs of anger or violence.

In July 1982, my Grandma Nau passed away. My family had to travel to Omaha, Nebraska for the funeral. I think we were all nervous because we didn't know how Ricky would act. I was concerned about being in a car with him for sixteen hours. I dreaded he would start a fight or get paranoid and run when we stopped at a gas station.

While Ricky did get a little anxious sitting in the car, overall he did pretty well. He didn't like anyone touching him, so I had to make sure that I was at least two inches away from him when we were sitting in the backseat. The continuing effort got uncomfortable and annoying after awhile. However, I did not want to trigger a bad reaction either.

While in Omaha, we visited relatives and went to a park for a family picnic. Ricky mostly stayed quiet and sat in the corner or away from people. He didn't interact very well, which was fine; I would rather him be quiet than to say to people that he saw demons or monsters. You would never know what words might come out of Ricky's mouth; so needless to say, we were always concerned, especially when we were around people other than the immediate family.

School was starting in a couple of weeks — and I was really excited. It was the beginning of my junior year. I was thrilled to be at Arapahoe High School back with my old friends, plus excited about meeting new friends and, of course, checking out new boys.

We had finished our summer cheerleading practices, and we were preparing for the first football game. I was hoping that going back to school would give me a little peace, comfort and an opportunity to escape problems at home. I also looked forward to having fun and getting Ricky off my mind.

The first couple of weeks of school went great. I had fun, I liked my classes, and I enjoyed the whole atmosphere that Arapahoe provided. I felt that there was a bunch of really great kids who went to this school. I felt good about that — and for the first time, I had an opportunity to fit in. However, keeping Ricky off my mind was practically impossible because he was becoming sicker and sicker.

Out of the blue, Ricky stopped eating and talking. The only thing he drank was juice. "Ricky, what's wrong? Why won't you eat?" Mom repeatedly asked.

Rick would not respond. With a worried tone, my mom refused to give up and pleaded, "Please Rick, tell me what's going on."

Ricky grabbed a piece of paper and wrote on it: "I can't talk or eat. They told me that they will attack you and everyone if I do."

Mom instantly knew he was talking about the voices. "Are these good or evil voices telling you this?" she asked.

Ricky wrote: "Evil. I'm scared. I have to do what they say."

In a gentle and loving voice, Mom kept talking to Ricky and said, "The voices can't hurt you or me or anyone else," she tenderly reassured him. "Don't be afraid. Rick, if you go to the doctors and get on some medication, it will help the voices go away. Don't you want them to go away?"

Ricky wrote: "Yes, but I can't eat."

With each passing day, everyone tried to convince Ricky to eat and not listen to the voices. By his face and eye expression, we could tell he wanted to believe us but he was scared. Because he didn't eat, Ricky continued to become weak and thin. This problem continued for almost a month. My parents tried to get him to go to the doctors but he would not listen or go. He would only write: "No, they will get me if I go."

I don't think the average person can understand a problem like this. With a child you just pick him up and take him to the doctor. You can't do that with an adult. Nor can you convince him what he should do. He is completely irrational and beyond reason.

Ricky also became more paranoid. He would not leave the house and most times, wouldn't leave the basement living room. One day, in a weak and quiet voice, Ricky made a comment to Bruce, Mom and me, "The neighbors are after me — and they are communists. They want us to burn."

I immediately responded, "No, Ricky. They are not after you or the family. They like you and care about you."

My mom and Bruce agreed, but Ricky would not listen and shook his head "no." After that, Ricky lay in his bed for days, in and out of trances. My parents were exhausted and scared for him. They constantly checked on him to make sure he was okay. Not one day went by where my parents did not plead with him to go to the hospital or to see the doctors. Ricky just ignored them. It was like watching innocent animal suffer when you couldn't help it.

Only once did I hear Ricky quietly speak about outer space and other worlds.

"Aliens say not to eat salt. There are other worlds where demons are rulers. My body is in outer space, and aliens have my brain," he emphatically stated with such conviction one had not doubt he believed it.

I tried to persuade him otherwise, "Ricky, please let Mom and Dad help you. You need medication. The aliens don't have your brain."

Once again, he shook his head "no."

Right before Labor Day in 1982, my brother Bruce found Ricky lying in his bed in a comatose-like state. He would not respond. Bruce got scared and ran upstairs and said to me in an upset voice, "Ricky is bad; we need to do something! Where's Mom?"

"She's outside," I said.

I ran downstairs to see Ricky while Bruce went outside to tell my mom. Ricky was hardly breathing and very pale. He was completely out of it and not able to make complete sentences. I tried talking to him, "Rick, you need help. Please let us help you."

He softly mumbled to me, "I die... I die... not eating. I want to... kill... eat... myself... die."

I knew he was trying to tell me he was killing himself by not eating. My mom came rushing down the stairs with Bruce. She was in tears and cried, "We need to get this boy to the hospital."

We all agreed.

Just the day before, Mom had heard from a friend that there was a good doctor who handled schizophrenics out of Boulder. She rushed back upstairs to get the number out of the phone book. She called him in desperation, pleading for an immediate appointment. We bowed our heads in relief when he said, "Yes."

My brother Bruce and I started to help Ricky. We told Ricky, "We are going to help you get out of bed. We are going to get you some help. Rick, we need to touch you to help you."

I almost burst into tears when I touched him. He was so frail. I could see bones sticking out of his shoulders. I was only inches from his face, and I could see in his eyes how sad he was and how lifeless he felt. He looked at me, and there was a small tear in his eye. I wanted so badly to hug him and tell him it was going to be okay. But I was afraid I would start crying — and we needed to stay focused on helping him.

Ricky did not like people touching him, and he freaked out if they did. So, Bruce and I had to be extremely careful with helping him up. We both put one of his arms around our necks so he felt like he was touching us and not us touching him. I remember glancing over at Bruce, and we both had a certain acknowledgment in our eyes that this was serious — and we had to be careful. As we were helping Ricky stand up, I couldn't help it. I had to rub his back for a few moments. I did see a sense of gratitude in his eyes. This was the only time he allowed me to touch him.

As we slowly walked Ricky upstairs, my mom made a comment, "Let's get him to the car. I have the car door open and ready to go." At that moment, Ricky finally realized we were going to take him to the doctors. He freaked out! He pushed us back and ran out of the house. I have no idea where he got the strength to run. It was unbelievable! Ricky's fears caused the adrenaline to kick in and off he went.

We knew we had to get him back into the house or to the car. "I'm going to go get a rope and tie him up!" Bruce yelled with a frantic voice. "We are taking him to the doctor!" Bruce was so frustrated with Ricky. He just wanted to get him some help.

The more Bruce tried to get close to Ricky, the more Ricky ran around the backyard. "Come on, Rick, we can help! Don't run! I don't want to tie you up! Let's just go to the car and go to the doctors. They can help."

Rick yelled back in fear, "No! Stay away from me!"

Mom knew this was not working so she told Bruce, "Stop, leave him alone. Put the rope down."

It finally came to the point where it was better to back off and get Ricky back into the house where he could be safe. Maybe somehow we could talk him into eating and getting him to settle down, so we could take him to the doctors the next day. Mom had to call the doctor back to cancel the appointment for that day. She asked if she could come in the next day.

"Ricky is probably too far gone for normal treatment," said the doctor. "I don't think I can help." Basically in so many words he said, "Don't call back."

Mom was crushed! That's not what a parent wants to hear about her child. It breaks my heart to think how she must have felt. She was hoping that this man might be or prayed he might be her son's savior. It makes me so mad, so let's name him "Doctor Moron."

That evening my mom and dad coaxed Ricky into eating some food. Once he started eating, he realized how hungry he was. They both kept encouraging him to eat the food so he could get his physical health back. We all were supporting him and letting him know the voices were wrong. We kept telling him, "We will be okay. They won't hurt us."

Once he saw we were okay and nothing was happening, he started to eat more. Thank goodness! A month of him not eating had taken its toll on everyone. We were bone weary of trying to convince him that something was not happening, that nobody was talking to him. It is like trying to bail out of the ocean.

A week after Labor Day, my dad came home from work and found Ricky standing in the middle of a circle of burning candles. He was in our basement in the middle of living room in a trance-like state. "Rick, what are you doing?" he asked.

Ricky just stared and didn't respond.

"Rick, are you okay? How long have you been here?"

Ricky's voice was weak and absent. "I don't know."

"What are you doing, Rick?" my dad asked again.

"Watching spirits come in and out of my body," he said quietly.

Based on the large size of the candles, and how far burned down they were, my dad knew he had been standing there for hours.

Dad was very upset and asked, "Why are you burning the candles, Rick?"

He looked at my dad in disbelief as if he should have known and replied, "To keep the evil spirits away."

"Rick, I need to put the candles out. They are almost done and I don't want a house fire."

"No!" Ricky said with frustration.

"I'm sorry, Rick, but I need to put them out. It will be okay. I want you come upstairs with me." Dad gently stated.

"I don't want to, the evil spirits will get me."

"They won't get you, Rick. You will be protected upstairs, if you come with me." My dad was trying to encourage Ricky to leave the circle of candles. I don't know how Dad managed it, but he talked Ricky into following him upstairs.

By this time, it was early evening. I had gotten home from school and Charlie had just gotten home from work. Ricky started to hallucinate much more than normal. He was speaking sporadically and making lots of weird comments about the evil spirits.

Ricky was getting very upset and telling Dad, "The evil spirits are all around me. They are coming in and out of my body! My brain! My ears! My eyes! They're in my head!"

Dad became very worried and called Mom. She rushed home from work. When she got home, Dad explained to her what had happened. Again, in an endless string of crisis another was upon us. My parents decided to call the police. Ricky was badly hallucinating and talking nonstop about the evil spirits and aliens.

When the police arrived my parents went out to the front yard. They explained the situation with Ricky to the police and what had been happening. When the police entered the house, Ricky saw them; he tried to run into the backyard. The police chased him and were able to get him down onto the ground and put handcuffs on him. They called the ambulance to come and take him to the hospital. Thank God! I was so relieved when the police showed up. We were finally getting some help. I think there was relief in everyone's eyes.

Ricky was taken to the Veterans Hospital for the second time. My parents followed the ambulance over to the hospital to help get Ricky admitted. While they were waiting in the admission room, Ricky became tearful and agitated. He did not want to be there. He would continuously brush or slap invisible things away from his head or legs. Eventually, Ricky tried to bolt out of the hospital and had to be caught by my dad and two guards. Ricky kept trying to hit and kick my dad as the guards held him.

"Let me go! I don't need to be here! I hate you!" Rick yelled.

With exhaustion, Dad shook his head and didn't respond. The guards handcuff him and place him on a seventy-two hour mental- health hold.

Ricky had a difficult time in the hospital. He would not cooperate and take his medication. He spit it out or hid it under his tongue. The nurses could not force him to take the pill. Ricky walked around the halls with his body in a crooked position. From what the nurses told us he thought demons were all around him and the other patients. He thought walking crooked kept them away.

Ricky wouldn't sleep in his bed; he would only sleep underneath the bed. He had terrible night terrors. He only felt safe from the evil worlds if he slept under the bed. He also thought all the food was poisoned and would not eat it. Ricky also became quarrelsome with other patients. The hospital staff felt he was a danger to himself and others, so they put him in lockdown for a few days.

When Ricky got out of lockdown, Mom went to the hospital to visit him. Days before when she had talked to him on the phone, Ricky asked her to bring some incense and fruit. "Why do you need incense, Rick?" asked Mom.

"To burn the demons away," he stated with agitation.

"Rick, I can't bring incense into the hospital, it's a fire hazard," she tried to explain.

He got mad and hung up on her.

On her way to the hospital, Mom stopped at the store to pick up some fruit. She knew Ricky had not been eating, and the nurses had given her permission to bring it. When my mom arrived at the hospital, she went into the visiting room to wait for Ricky.

As Ricky entered the visiting room, Mom knew instantly Ricky was quarrelsome. "Did you bring my fruit? Where is it?" Ricky yelled at Mom.

"Don't you think you could say 'hello' first, Rick?" Mom stated with a matter-of-fact tone as she laid the bag of fruit on the table.

"Where is my incense?" he yelled again.

"I did not bring you incense, Rick. You are not allowed incense in the hospital. I already told you that," she said nervously.

Ricky got mad, walked over to the table, and grabbed the bag. He opened it up to see if there was any incense. "I told you Rick, I did not bring incense," she said with reservation.

When he realized there was only fruit, he grabbed a peach and threw it hard against the wall. My mom jumped up in fear, "What in the world are you doing, Rick?"

"I told you to bring incense! I need to burn the demons!" he screamed.

The nurses heard Ricky scream so they came into the room. At that time, Ricky was very upset and kicked a wooden chair over. "There are evil spirits on this chair," he yelled at the nurses. Ricky left the room.

The nurse gently said to Mom, "I think it's best you go, Mrs. Nau; Ricky is not doing well this evening."

My mom agreed and left the hospital without saying goodbye to Ricky. His anger and violent behavior were starting to intensify.

During this time, Ricky also escaped the hospital. We don't know the circumstances in which he managed to escape. The hospital would not tell us; but he ran away, and the hospital had to go find him and bring him back. He was only gone for a few hours. It is interesting that he was able to get out of the hospital when you consider he was supposed to be on a locked floor. Furthermore, with Ricky showing more violent behavior, why wasn't he watched more closely? These are questions my parents asked the hospital, but they could not get any answers.

Since Ricky was being difficult and not taking his medication the majority of the time, the hospital had to get a court order from the judge to give him medication. Ricky tried to represent himself to fight it, but he lost. Thank goodness! At least the judge recognized how sick Ricky was and how badly he needed medication. This order allowed the hospital to give Ricky medication without his approval.

One night in November 1982, my mom and I went to see Ricky at the hospital. He asked Mom to stop by the store and pick up some food for him that was in containers. Ricky said, "If the food is in a container, evil spirits cannot poison it."

"Okay, Rick, I will get you some food," she stated without argument. She agreed with him because she did not want to ruin our visit.

I remember the car ride to the hospital was very quiet. My mom didn't say much. I'm sure it was hard for her to go there. I personally was feeling sick to my stomach, my hands were sweating, and I was scared to go the hospital. I'm not really sure why I felt that way. I guess I didn't know what to expect from the psych ward. What type of environment would it be? What type of people would I see? Were they as sick as Ricky? There was a deep sense of sadness in me knowing that I was going to see my very ill brother, and I wasn't sure if the doctors would ever be able to help him.

The visit with Ricky was very short. He didn't seem interested in seeing us, but was only interested in getting his container of food. He mumbled comments that he was part Jesus and part alien mastermind of the universe. He talked a lot about the demons and insects walking around the hospital. How the aliens were going to take over our world. How he had a battle between good and evil from his right side to his left side. He also spoke a lot about the poisoned food and water there in the hospital. My mom and I just patiently listened to what was after all insane rambling.

Seeing Ricky sitting there at the table looking up toward the ceiling as though he was talking to someone else was the first time I really realized that he was never going to be normal again. No matter what had happened up to this point, I had a fantasy in my mind that he was going to be cured or helped. My heart sank with this realization that he was no longer the brother that I grew up with. I knew that even if he took his medication, it would not heal his disease; it would only mask it and maybe ease the symptoms. How terrible can this be to lose your mind to an unreal world that does not exist?

When Mom and I left the hospital that night, it started to lightly snow and rain. For some reason, it seemed really dark outside. I knew in my heart, it would be the first and last time I would visit Ricky in this hospital. I did not want to go back. It made me too sad. The car ride home was very quiet. Looking out the side window I masked my tears from my mom. I didn't want her to see my pain because she had enough of her own.

CHAPTER FIVE

Where Fear Exists, Happiness Does Not

L ooking back over the fall of 1982, it went pretty well after Ricky was admitted to the Veterans Hospital. It was a relief to have him in the doctor's care and to give my family a break. School went well. I kept up good grades, and I was meeting a lot of new people. Of course, there were a few cute boys I had crushes on and enjoyed watching them as they walked down the hall, but it was not worth pursuing because I didn't want to deal with a boyfriend with all my family issues. I was not mentally or emotionally in the right place to have a boyfriend. I had no ability to open up or be close with someone new. I was afraid they would judge me if they knew about my brother. I just wanted to keep people at a distance. I wanted keep my fear and frustrations to myself, to keep my family a secret.

I did go to homecoming with a really close friend named Brian. We had lots of fun and enjoyed ourselves. It was nice going as friends because there were no expectations. Brian always made me feel safe and comfortable. We were good friends since seventh grade and he always treated me with respect. Brian helped me to forget about Ricky's illness for a night. He made me laugh and dance. I don't think Brian ever knew how much it meant to me, to have that release, because my days and nights were only filled with concern for my family, my brother and my homework.

In December 1982, we had the State Championship Cheerleading/Pom competition. The competition was intense. There were a lot of schools participating at all levels (2A though 4A). My school was a 4A level. In the morning, as I was getting ready for the competition, Ricky called. I spoke with him for a few minutes and then I had to hand the phone over to my mom because I couldn't listen to what he was saying anymore.

Ricky kept yelling at me, "You're fake, or evil, you're an imposter, I hate you. God's is going to punish you if you keep sending me your evil vibes." I didn't even respond, I was too tired to argue with him.

I was angry because he started my day off on a bad note. I had to go cheer, put a smile on my face and be happy for the competition. How was I going to go do that, when I was feeling hurt and down? My squad was really good and I knew we had a great chance to win. During the competition, as I was yelling the words, I felt this huge release of emotion. The louder I yelled, the more emotion was released. I think I was subconsciously yelling my anger and frustrations toward Ricky, so I yelled as loud as I could! Afterwards, I could hardly speak and my voice was hoarse. It felt great to yell, and I needed it. The rest of the day went great and my squad won first place. It was nice to bring home the state trophy.

A week later, I felt light and in good spirits. I think all that yelling really was therapeutic for me. I asked another close friend name Scott to the Winter Sadie Hawkins dance. We had a great time! I felt happy and we danced all night long. Scott was a joy to be around because he was always in a good mood and had a positive attitude. Not once, did I think about Ricky. I was determined not allow him to ruin my evening. Looking back now, it was the last time I really felt happy and had a fun time in high school.

On the other hand, for my parents, I think the stress of worrying about Ricky the last ten months took its toll. I noticed a distance developing between them. They didn't seem to get along very well. While Ricky was in the hospital, they would go visit him separately. I don't blame them for feeling frustrated and hurt. I'm not sure if they were blaming each other for his illness, or if they were feeling some type of guilt. They both seemed to be on different pages, and working through their own stress and feelings separately. It is hard to have a child who is mentally sick, and there is no cure for schizophrenia. So what do you do as a parent? How do you deal with knowing your child will never be better? How do you find the right care for him or her? Especially when society still wants to ignore mental illness.

Over the last few months, Mom had read a lot of books and magazines about schizophrenia. She also tried to watch every television show that had any topics regarding mental illness. She tried to learn and find ways to help Ricky. She saw that there was going to be a seminar in town on vitamin treatments for mental illness hosted by Dr. Carl Pfeiffer. My mom went to the seminar to learn about Dr. Pfeiffer's studies on schizophrenia and how he had started a clinic/research center known as the Princeton Bio-Brain Center in New Jersey. The concept of the clinic was to test hair, blood and urine to discover deficiencies in the body and use Mega-Vitamin Orthomolecular Treatment to resolve or help schizophrenia and other disorders. My mom called them immediately to schedule a meeting for Ricky to be tested at the beginning of February.

Ricky was released from the Veterans Hospital at the end of

December of '82. He came home feeling a little better, looking better, and having gained weight. He took his medication and did okay. The medication did have some bad side effects; however, it was better than not taking it at all. Ricky was easier to handle and be around when he was on medication. The only concern was that Ricky promised my dad he would only take medication until they went to New Jersey.

In early February of '83, my parents took Ricky to New Jersey to meet the doctors at the Princeton Bio-Brain Center. My parents were concerned about traveling with Ricky. I think he was willing to go because he too had high hopes that this center would be able to help him. Overall, Ricky did okay traveling. He wasn't feeling good — and he felt insecure, but he stayed close to my parents. He also lacked some basic reasoning skills, so my parents had to watch him closely. Ricky was still paranoid against other ethnic groups, and my parents were afraid he would say or do something against other ethnicities. They never let him out of their sight or more than an arm's length away.

The doctors examined Ricky and did a urine test, blood work and hair analysis. They showed my parents the results, and they came up with a whole mega-vitamin plan they felt would work for Ricky

Ricky in New Jersey visiting the Princeton Bio-Brain Center

based on all of his medical results. Ricky was excited about starting the vitamin plan and so were my parents. They had high hopes that maybe they could help balance Ricky's brain by bringing up the levels of vitamin B6. The theory at the time was schizophrenics tend to have low levels of vitamin B6 in their bodies.

Ricky immediately followed the doctor's orders and started taking the vitamins. As soon as my parents and Ricky got back to the hotel, Ricky was excited and ripped open the vitamin bottles. He started taking way too many vitamins.

"Ricky, slow down. The doctor told you to start with a little and build up," Mom cautioned with concern.

"I want to get better," Ricky said, excited.

"I understand, but you're going to make yourself sick!" Mom tried to explain and slow Ricky down.

While she didn't want to ruin his excitement, she knew he would get an upset stomach. Hours later, Ricky did get sick. He basically overdosed on vitamins. Ricky remained ill for the next couple of days while they flew back from New Jersey.

After they returned, Ricky stayed excited and continued to take the vitamins for a few weeks. Unfortunately, schizophrenia has a vicious disease cycle. As soon as schizophrenics start feeling better, they tend to quit taking the medication because they don't think they need it anymore. Schizophrenics cannot comprehend that they are sick nor understand it's the medication that makes them feel better. They usually think they got better on their own — and they do not need to take the medication. So, they quit taking it. They have a tendency to think everyone else is sick. That is why it is so hard to get a schizophrenic to take medications; it's the lack of reasoning and understanding that they only feel better because of the medication. They don't get that the "cause" (schizophrenia) causes the outcome (hallucinations and voices). It's impossible to rationalize or explain that to a schizophrenic.

This is what happened with Ricky in regards to the vitamins, and of course, all the medications. Since he was doing better, he decided that he was not ill and no longer needed to take any vitamins.

One morning, Ricky woke up in nasty mood. My mom was getting ready to leave for work and gave him his vitamins.

"I'm not taking this!" Ricky stated in annoyed manner.

As my mom got frustrated she told Ricky, "Rick, we have been through this before. You are only feeling better because of the vitamins! Take the vitamins!"

"No!" Ricky said as he swiped her hand away and all the vitamins fell to the floor.

"I am not going to argue with you, Ricky," Mom said firmly. "Pick up all the vitamins off the floor now!" she demanded in an angry tone.

Ricky picked up the vitamins and he yelled at her, "I'm not taking them! I don't need them! You're sick, not me!"

Mom switched tones and calmly tried to persuade Ricky into taking the vitamins. "Ricky, don't you remember what the doctor said? He told you that this was a process and a way of life. You have to be consistent and take the vitamins every day for them to help you. Don't you want to continue to feel better?"

Ricky stomped out of the kitchen and went downstairs yelling, "No! Leave me alone. I know what I'm doing."

Mom had to leave for work. She just shook her head and said to me, "Not again! Why can't I get this kid to listen?"

"Because he is sick," I quietly replied.

My mom shook her head with acknowledgment. We both left for the day, knowing that Ricky would never take the vitamins again. It made us sad because our hope that somehow Ricky was going to get better was once again shattered.

By March of '83, Ricky had stopped taking all vitamins and medication. My parents tried everything to get him back onto medication. They tried persuasion, begging, crying, bribing him with clothes, trips, money or movies - anything to get him to see a doctor, but Ricky would not cooperate.

He started to hallucinate more often. He would see us kids turn into monsters, insects or creatures, and Dad turn into a dragon. It was terrifying for Ricky because it was all so real to him. At times, he would run from us or hide because he saw horns coming out of our heads. If he was not scared, he would come around and poke us to see if we were real; or he would swipe his hand over the top our heads to get rid of the horns or evil spirits. I personally could not comprehend or understand what he was seeing — he lived in such an unreal world. That is why it was so heartbreaking to watch.

The journey with Ricky had turned into an emotional roller-coaster ride. One week there was hope that a doctor, medication or new procedure might help him. The next week, we felt sadness and depression, as we knew he would never get better. It was starting to take a heavy toll on everyone. I was beginning to withdraw from school and my grades were declining. I still went out with my friends, but I never had a good time. Unable to tell anyone what was going on at home, I had to act fake and happy and that alone was stressful. With all the acting that I was doing, I should have become an actress. I had lots of practice.

During my high school spring break, I was at home alone with Ricky. Most of the day, Ricky just stared at me and made me feel very uncomfortable. I could tell he had hallucinations by the way he looked at me. One minute he seemed scared of me, and the next minute he was mad at me. I tried to avoid him because I didn't want to aggravate him.

Later that afternoon, I started to get a little hungry so I went into the kitchen. Ricky was sitting at the kitchen table by the door. As I walked in, Ricky jumped up and pushed me hard into the refrigerator. I lost my balance, fell forward, and hit my cheekbone on the refrigerator door handle.

"What are you doing?" I yelled.

"Your spirits are bugging me again!" he said angrily. Ricky started to poke me in the shoulder, so I pushed him away. "Leave me alone! Stop touching me!" I demanded.

I got frustrated and annoyed. I was not in the mood to deal with him. As I walked toward the cupboard, Ricky kept swiping his hand above my head to get rid of the demons or insects he saw.

"Stop it, Rick! You're hallucinating," I cried.

Ricky ignored me, and then he proceeded to hit me hard on the top of my head as if he was killing a bug or something.

I backed up and screamed at him, "Don't ever hit me again! I'm sick and tired of you always poking and pushing me! Why can't you understand that you are sick? You need help!" I vented my anger toward his illness as I continued to yell at him, "Why can't you take your medication? Why can't you listen to Mom and Dad?"

Ricky yelled back, "I'm not ill! You guys are trying to make me ill. They told me that you are evil! The demon bugs are going into your head."

"I'm not evil! It's part of your illness. You need help!" I yelled, trembling.

He spit out his usual hostile words, "You're an evil person with a black brain! Your bad energy is bugging me! Leave me alone! Stay away from me!"

I knew I had to get out of the kitchen and calm down, so I started to walk to the back door to go outside. Ricky pushed my back as I walked away, and said, "If you don't leave me alone, I'm going to kill you."

I stumbled a little bit and I hit the corner of the oven handle with my side, but I kept walking to the door. I did not respond or look at him. Not wanting to push the argument any further because I was alone with him. I went outside to the backyard and sat down on the lounge chair to cry. I kept thinking, *"why, God? Why can't my family be normal like we use to be? Why can't Ricky get better?"*

I felt angry, scared and frustrated. I didn't know what to say or do. At that time, I didn't believe in my heart he would hurt me, but I was starting to rethink that and I became terrified. A few minutes later, my dad got home from work. I told him what had happened and that Ricky had threatened to kill me.

Dad was upset so he went downstairs to find Ricky. As he entered Ricky's bedroom, he found him holding a pistol. "What are you doing with a gun?" Dad demanded.

"I just bought it," Ricky said.

"Give me the gun," Dad said his voice shaking.

Ricky handed the gun to him.

"Where did you get this gun?" Dad questioned.

"At the sporting goods store up the street," Ricky replied.

"When did you buy this gun?" Dad demanded but curious.

"A couple of days ago," Ricky said in a sad voice.

"You can't have this gun. I'm taking it back," my dad said as he put the gun back into the case.

"I tried to take it back to the store, but they told me I couldn't return it," Ricky tried to explain.

"They better take it back!" said Dad as he stormed out of Ricky's room with the gun case in hand.

My father was very upset — especially since Ricky was mentally ill and had the capability to buy a gun. I personally don't believe that Ricky ever tried to take the gun back. I do believe that he originally bought the gun to kill himself. However, after that day, I had enlightenment moment and I started to realize that Ricky did indeed have the potential to hurt someone beside himself.

Later that evening, my dad told Mom what happened. She was just as angry as Dad. "Take the gun back and yell at them!" she demanded.

Dad thoroughly agreed. He took the gun back that night to the sporting goods store. As he walked up to the counter, he said in a very controlled, angry way, "I'm here to bring this gun back! You guys sold this gun to my son who is mentally ill!"

"Sorry sir, we can't take back returned guns," said the salesman.

"Yes, you can!" said Dad, his face turning crimson.

"No sir, we can't take guns back," the salesman said again.

"Oh, yes you can! It's against the law to sell a gun to a mentally ill person. You take it back now or I will report it to the appropriate authorities because it's against the law!"

Dad was smoldering at this point.

Frantically the salesman said, "Yes, sir," and returned the cash. The salesman sensed the store could get in trouble and that my dad was not to be reckoned with.

A few weeks later it was Easter, and Ricky started to live more in his unreal world than in reality. He was very moody on Easter Day and argued with everyone. It seemed like he was constantly trying to start a fight. Colorado had a bad snowstorm a couple days before and we were all stuck inside with four feet of new snow.

Dealing with Ricky was draining. We always had to be on guard and watch what we said and did to avoid triggering any violent episodes. We never knew what would trigger Ricky to hit or slap someone, which became more frequent.

This particular day, my brother Bruce got up to go change the TV channel, and Ricky got so mad, he jumped up out of the chair, charged Bruce, and hit him as hard has he could in the chest. Bruce fell back but caught himself on the TV. I thought for sure Bruce was going to knock him out. Bruce was 6'2" and well built, while Ricky was only 5'10" and very thin.

Thank goodness Bruce kept his composure and didn't respond. I was really afraid there was going to be a big fight, and we wouldn't be able to get the police there because of the snow. Both my brother Charlie and I immediately stood up next to Bruce, and yelled at Ricky, "Get out of here!" We all stood there looking at him until Ricky left the room. He knew he could not fight all three of us.

Both my parents sensed something had happened and came into the room asking, "What's wrong?"

We all snapped at once, "Nothing!"

We were all frustrated and didn't want my parents to start another fight with Ricky.

We knew we had to stick together and protect each other. Bruce was a little miffed because once again Ricky had hit him, and he could not do anything about it. As Bruce went to sit down on the couch, I remember telling him, "I'm proud of you for not responding. If you did, it could have turned out a lot worse."

Bruce just shrugged and muttered, "Yeah."

As we waited for Easter dinner to be done, I watched Bruce as he kept rubbing his chest. I knew Ricky had hurt him but Bruce would not admit it. Needless to say, Easter dinner wasn't enjoyable!

In the meantime, school was school. I tried to focus on homework, which was becoming harder for me. It was prom time and a friend asked me to go but I turned him down. I wasn't interested in getting dressed up. I felt depressed and had a negative attitude. Trying to be kind I said no and that I had a family obligation. It was a lame excuse and we both knew it. I didn't have the heart to tell him that my family's obligation was really a serious family issue. I figured he wouldn't understand and that it was best to keep my family's secret.

It was also time for cheerleading and pom tryouts again. I

wasn't excited about tryouts. I was afraid my negative attitude might prevent me from making the squad. I'm sure they could tell I was distracted and not enthused. I went ahead and tried out for the cheerleading squad again, and despite my attitude, I did make the team. Deep in my heart I did enjoy cheering at the games, it was always fun. It definitely helped me take my mind off Ricky for a few hours. I was pleasantly surprised that my new cheer squad voted me as co-captain. It was a great feeling for me that they actually liked me — I was feeling pretty down those days. Even though it wasn't a big deal to the other girls, it was big deal for me. I needed something positive. They had no idea how it affected me and how important it was to me since I was feeling so depressed about Ricky. I also felt out of place because I didn't like being at home, and I had nowhere to go — and I didn't have anyone to talk to. At that time, I felt like I should have lived on the "Island of Misfit Toys." No one could understand the world that my family and I were living in.

Things continued to get worse through April of '83. Ricky became angrier and more emotional. My mom called many doctors and tried to get medication, but they would not prescribe medication without seeing Ricky first. Of course, we could not get Ricky to go to the doctors. He ran away if we even mentioned it. It was a bad catch-22. No medication, no help. No help, no medication.

One evening I stood at the sink doing dishes while everyone else was in the living room watching TV. I didn't hear Ricky come up the stairs from the basement. All of sudden, he came up behind me, grabbed the back of my neck, and put a hunting knife up to my throat. Petrified, I could not move or speak.

He whispered in my ear in a raspy, unreal tone, "How nice it would be to cut your neck and see you bleed to death." He then pushed the knife into my skin and then slowly moved it across my neck without cutting me. His laugh was evil, very chilling. It was like the devil was inside of him. I had never heard that laugh before — it made the hairs on the back of my neck stand up.

Frantically I pushed his arm away and started to scream, "Mom! Mom!"

My mom and my brothers Charlie and Bruce rushed into the kitchen. "What's wrong?" Mom asked, now panicky.

"Ricky put a knife to my neck," I managed to say with tears welling up.

By that time, Ricky had backed up and just laughed. He told my mom and brothers, "I was only teasing her."

With more trepidation than anger, she yelled, "Richard, that is not funny! Give me the knife! You don't behave that way in this house!"

I guarantee you, he was not teasing! I have no doubt in my mind, if no one was home, he would have cut my throat. Charlie and Bruce walked me into the living room and sat with me to watch TV. I did not cry because I wanted to be tough, but the tears welled up in my eyes for hours and I could hardly see the TV.

Later that night my mom asked me, "Are you okay?"

Softly I said, a sad, "Yeah."

"I'm sorry, I just don't know what to do," she said with disappointment.

"Why can't we have him committed to some hospital?" I asked desperately.

"It's against the law, we can't commit him, the courts system has to do it," Mom said.

"Can't we please ask a doctor to go to the courts," I pleaded.

"I can't get Ricky to go the doctor or have a doctor evaluate him long enough to make that decision," she said, her frustration mounting.

"I feel like our hands are tied and there is no one around to help."

"I know, Mom," I said. I sadly got up, and went to my bedroom sobbing.

Later that night, my mom went through all the kitchen drawers and pulled out all the sharp knives and scissors and hid them.

By this time, Ricky living at home was a major undertaking that put enormous stress and strain on my family; however, my parents had no options. He was their son, and they loved him. They couldn't just kick him out. I do applaud them for trying to help him, but at the same time, it tore us all apart. My parents did the best they could to be aware of all the other kids' needs. I have no doubt if any of us kids told my parents they wanted Ricky out of the house, they would have listened and responded; but none of us did. We all knew Ricky had nowhere else to go, and there was no place for mentally ill people to live.

Our ability to cope with Ricky's illness was starting to diminish.

It was the beginning of May '83, and I had a few weeks of school left. This year was not turning out as I had hoped. I felt more isolated than ever. Home wasn't home, and I no longer felt safe there. I was scared in my own house and I never wanted to be alone. I always kept my bedroom door locked at night.

Ricky started to believe that all my friends were bad too. He told me, "Your friends are devils. They are prostitutes and evil. I believe your friend Stacy is a communist. She is out to destroy my brain."

"No they're not, Rick," I said, irritated. "How many times do you we have to tell you its part of your illness? You're just being paranoid!" I don't know why I even tried to explain it since he never listened or believed me. Once Ricky got an idea in his mind, he did not let it go.

I started to also notice that if any of my friends came to pick me up, Ricky acted angry. He stomped around the house and slammed the front door after they walked in. He also stared at them as if he was about to go into attack mode.

A fear was growing inside me that Ricky was going to hurt one of my friends. He particularly didn't like any of my friends who had blond hair, especially Stacy. He thought that was a sign of being imposters — and they were all really the devil in disguise.

I knew it was best not to have friends come over to the house anymore. If I did go out with my friends, I either waited outside on the front porch or I asked them to pick me up on the corner of my parents' street. I couldn't risk that chance of Ricky hurting them. If my friends did happen to show up at my house unexpectedly, I rushed out of the house quickly so they would not have time to get out of the car and come to the door. From that time on, I no longer allowed any friends inside my house.

I know they all wondered what was going on — and that it was weird they had to pick me up on the corner or see me rush out of the house. At first, I lied as to why I was on the corner, but eventually I told them a little bit about what was happening with Ricky. Not much, but a just enough to explain my actions.

"My brother is sick and a little weird" was my standard explanation. "He gets upset easily. It's best not to be around him." However, I didn't have the heart to tell them how serious it was or how afraid I was for all of us.

One afternoon, after school, I was lying on the couch watching TV with my brother Bruce. Ricky paced back and forth very aggressively in the dining room. He kept looking at us and shaking his head as if he was very annoyed with us. He talked to himself and said weird things in an alien language. We could not understand any of the words he said. I watched Ricky go back into the bathroom and didn't think much of it.

Within a few minutes, he ran out of the bathroom with a towel wrapped around his head like a turban and jumped on top of me. He started punching me in the face.

"Stop! Stop!" I screamed.

"You're the devil! The devil is inside of you! You are evil!" Ricky kept yelling with such determination and outrage toward me.

I tried blocking his punches with my arms and hands, but he was much stronger than me.

My brother Bruce instantly jumped up and tried to stop him. He got behind him and tried to pull him off as he yelled at him, "Stop! Get off her!"

My brother Charlie heard the commotion from the basement and ran upstairs to help Bruce pull Ricky off me.

Ricky finally stopped and accused me, "She is the devil! She is the devil!" He kept saying it over and over again as he pointed his finger at me.

Charlie and Bruce were dumbfounded. They just stood there and yelled at Ricky, "Leave her alone! She is not the devil!"

I ran into the bedroom and locked the door. I cried all night because for one moment in time, I actually believed Ricky. *"Was I the devil? Is the devil inside of me? Am I evil? Am I sending evil spirits? What was he seeing? Was it real? Are spirits really entering me? Oh my God. What's wrong with me? How could I think that? How could I let Ricky make me feel this way?"* I felt resentful and distressed. I allowed him to shake me to depths of my soul, I allowed him to make me question myself. "I hate you Ricky for making me feel this way!" I said out loud, as my angry thoughts turn to back to tears.

As I cried myself to sleep, I kept asking God, "Why does this have to happen?"

When I woke up the next morning, I had a black eye and a bruise on my cheek. I had to wear a lot of makeup to school. A couple of my close friends knew something had happened — I could tell by their concerned look and their raised eye brows, but they didn't ask, which I was grateful for. I know I would have broken down into tears if they did.

When my parents found out what happened, they told my brothers I was never to be alone with Ricky again. I always had to be with someone when I was at home. The fact was if Ricky attacked me again, I was not big enough or strong enough to fight him off. Everyone supported that decision.

If I knew nobody was going to be home after school, I would stay at school to study or go to a friend's house until someone was home. For some reason, Ricky started to focus more of his anger toward me and wanted to pick on me. He knew that both Charlie and Bruce were bigger than him, so he didn't focus as much attention on them.

Ricky always kept his eye on me wherever I was in the house. Every opportunity he had to hit me or punch me in the arm or on the head as I walked by, he would. I was starting to get to the point where I was becoming really pissed off. I wanted to hit him back, but I knew in my heart that he was waiting for that opportunity or reason to attack me again. No matter how hard it was to hold back, I could not allow him to hurt me again because the next time, it could be a lot worse.

It was the second weekend of May '83, and there was a big weekend party up at Daniels Park with big bonfires and lots of kids. As we neared graduation senior parties flourished. I decided to go with some friends and a few senior guys who I really didn't know that well.

Deep inside I felt furious with Ricky. I felt he invaded my space and privacy. Even though I wasn't with him, he was in my thoughts twenty-four hours a day. I consistently thought, *"Is he okay? Has he hurt himself? Is my family okay? Did he hurt them? How can we get him to the doctors? What can I say to make him understand?"*

I just needed a break from all these traumatic thoughts! I so badly needed to escape from Ricky!

I decided to drink at the party and cut loose. I just wanted to be free from all the frustration and fear. I was having a great time socializing with everyone, and I started to get a little drunk. By that time, a group of my friends decided to smoke some pot. I decided I wanted to smoke too. I thought it would be fun. I had never smoked pot, but that particular night, I wanted to try it. I just kept thinking I wanted to be free of problems and be a teenager again. I hadn't felt like a teenager for almost a year.

Smoking pot ended up being a really bad decision. I became paranoid and extremely depressed. I felt like I couldn't move because I was so paranoid that Ricky was coming to Daniels Park to kill me. I just froze.

My friends kept laughing and asking me, "What is wrong with you? Why are you being so paranoid?" I couldn't answer.

"Come on, let's go party some more," they insisted as they tried to pull me in the direction of the bonfire.

"No, I want to stay here. Please just leave me here," I said, scared.

"Okay," they said, laughing as they walked away.

Later on that night, as we were driving home, I got sick to my stomach. I was scared to go home. The closer we got to my house, the more upset I became. I didn't want to walk into the house late at night in the dark. I was afraid Ricky would be waiting for me, knife in hand.

I started to cry and I asked my friend, "Can I please spend the night at your house?"

"Of course. What's wrong? Why are you so upset?" she asked, confused.

"I just don't want to go home. I can't explain right now," I said in a shaky voice.

"Okay. Will your mom get upset?" she asked.

"No, I'll call her when we get to your house," I said gratefully.

When we got to her house, I called my mom to tell her I wasn't coming home. I never did explain to my friend why I got so upset. I just kept my mouth shut. I guess in a way, I felt embarrassed and didn't like showing how vulnerable I really felt.

Looking back now, I realize that smoking pot was the stupidest thing I could have ever done. I should have realized that pot was one of the factors that triggered Ricky's schizophrenia. I could have easily put myself at risk for becoming ill. It was a dumb call and I should have known better.

Graduation for the seniors of '83 had passed, and the juniors had a few days of school left. I was glad the year was about over, and I kept high hopes that my senior year would be great. It was summer, and softball was about to begin again. I was looking forward to playing and spending time with some of my friends who went to other high schools. We had a great team, and I knew we would win the championship again! It was a good way to start off the senior year. Plus, I was excited because my brother Jim was coming home in a couple of days. I was happy there would be another male in the house to help with Ricky. Maybe things would turn around. Ricky had always admired and listened to Jim. Maybe Jim could influence Ricky to get back on medication. Just maybe things would get better. Just maybe.

CHAPTER SIX

A Roller-Coaster Ride
that Doesn't Come Down

I was excited! My brother Jim had come home, and he was planning to stay through first of fall. In October he was going to head back to Seattle to go to herbology school. I was enthusiastic about spending some time with him. He was fifteen years older than me, and we'd never really had any opportunity to spend quality time together as adults. I had lots of questions for him. He'd served in Vietnam, and I wanted to know what his experience was like. I was eager for this chance to get to know him as a man and as my brother.

I think Jim noticed immediately that everyone's nerves were shot, and we were all walking on eggshells around Ricky. Jim decided to take Ricky camping in Utah over Memorial Day weekend with one of his friends. He wanted to give my parents a break. Personally, I was grateful. I was afraid of Ricky — and I was relieved he was going to be gone for a few days.

I don't think the camping trip turned out as well as Jim had hoped. Ricky was not cooperative, and he was very paranoid. Ricky did not want to hike around the area. He wanted to stay close to the campsite in fear that the devil would attack him.

"If I go over there, the devil will get into my head," Ricky told Jim.

Jim was always patient and said, "Ricky, the devil can't get you. It's all a part of your hallucinations. You have to trust me. Let's go hiking."

"No, I don't want to go," Ricky said with his eyes darting wildly.

"Okay, we will stay here then," said Jim.

Later in the evening when they were sitting around the campfire, Ricky started telling them about all the demons, the devil, and what they were going to do. "The devil tries to attack me at night," Ricky blurted out.

"Ricky, the devil isn't attacking you; it's part of your illness," Jim countered.

"If I don't listen, the devil will attack you and the family. The devil is powerful and rules the universe," said a thoroughly convinced Ricky.

"Ricky, if you take medication, you wouldn't have these feelings. Medication can help," said Jim.

He snarled back, "You don't know what you're talking about. The medication makes me sick. They told me not to take it! They said my brain will split and go into different universes."

"Who told you not to take it?" Jim asked.

This question only incited Ricky's anger. "The rulers of the universe! The demons and voices I hear! They said our family is bad and needs to be punished. If I take the medication, I can't help the family. I need to save you all from the demons."

"Ricky, part of schizophrenia is hearing voices that are not real and seeing hallucinations that are not real. You need to take medication to help stop the voices and stop the demons. Otherwise, I can't help you," Jim stated in a soft, calm voice full of reason.

"No! You don't get it! I'm not sick! You are!" Ricky yelled as he stood up.

"The demons are going to get you." His voice became cold and indifferent as he stood there staring at Jim.

"Okay, Rick, it's fine, just sit down. I'm not going to discuss it with you anymore," said Jim as he attempted to change the topic of conversation.

Jim knew he needed to take Ricky home the next day before Ricky's paranoia progressed into an out-of-control episode. Jim was sad, though, because he had hoped to have a successful conversation with Ricky about taking medication.

Yet Jim never stopped trying to reason with his brother about his illness. He never gave up on trying to persuade Ricky into taking medication. Unfortunately, Ricky would always turn on anyone who tried to help him. In his tortured mind he was convinced that you were the devil in disguise, and you were trying to talk him into believing he was sick.

After the camping trip, Ricky's attitude toward Jim started to change. He saw Jim as a threat, which was sad. All Jim wanted to do was help his little brother.

It was now the beginning of June '83. Every once in awhile we would try to get Ricky out of the house for some fresh air. My parents and Jim decided to take Ricky on a hike and dig for some quartz-crystal rocks up in Upper Bear Creek area. Ricky had always loved the mountains, and they thought that on such a beautiful, warm summer day, it would be good to get him out of the house for some exercise and to smell the fresh pine trees. So, full of hope they went out together that afternoon. Overall, the hike went pretty well. I think Ricky responded with a positive attitude to the hiking and exploring for the first part of the day. He was surprisingly not overly paranoid and able to be out among other people. The good day, however, did not end well. Toward the end of the hike, Ricky started to become aggravated.

Jim walked about fifteen feet in front of Ricky. Out of the blue, Ricky threw a hammer-pick (metal pick used for digging rocks) high up in the air and tried to hit Jim on the head. The hammer-pick missed Jim's head by a foot.

"What the hell are you doing!" screamed Jim and my dad at the same time, as they stopped and gasped at Ricky in disbelief.

Ricky shrugged.

"Ricky, you could have hurt him!" Mom cried out. "What are you thinking?"

Ricky did not respond again. He just kept walking.

"Don't ever do that again!" yelled Dad.

My dad snatched up the hammer-pick. Both of my parents and Jim were upset. I know that Ricky saw Jim turn into a monster or something like that, and he wanted to hurt him. If that hammer would have hit Jim on the head, it could have easily killed him. Needless to say, the car ride home was silent.

As summer was starting, I tried really hard to focus on cheerleading practices, softball games, and escapes to friends' houses. I just wanted to be out of the house. I couldn't wait for school to start, so I had a place to hang out away from the chaos of my home. I noticed I was becoming more agitated and moody, too. I often cried, felt frustrated, and was ready to explode. The stress was catching up to me.

One evening, I was in the kitchen doing dishes. Ricky surprised me once again. I turned around — and there he was standing directly behind me. He grabbed my neck and started choking me. I gasped for air. I grabbed his wrist and tried pulling his hands off my neck. He was so strong I couldn't budge him.

I tried to scream, "Stop! Help!" but my voice failed and words were silent gasps.

Gasping for air Ricky kept choking me and looking into my mouth. Finally, my brother Jim could hear commotion and my muted screams, and he ran into the kitchen.

"Rick, what are you doing?" Jim cried as he grabbed Ricky's wrist, trying desperately to pry his hands free of my neck.

Finally, Jim pulled him off, and they fell backwards a bit. I bent over, gasping and panting for breath.

"She has demons and bugs coming out of her mouth!" Ricky screamed, truly terrified.

"I don't care! You can't choke people because you are seeing hallucinations!" Jim yelled.

Bruce heard Jim and Ricky yelling, so he ran into the kitchen to see what was happening. Once again, I ran to my room crying.

Jim and my brother Bruce kept knocking on my bedroom door to see if I was okay.

"Leave me alone!" I cried and yelled at the door.

"Let us in. Are you okay?" they asked.

"No! I'm sick of this! Leave me alone!" I cried some more.

A couple of hours later, I looked into the mirror — and I had red marks all over my neck. The marks lasted for a couple of days. I had to wear high-collared shirts to cheerleading practice so no one would see the marks. I just couldn't take it anymore! I loved Ricky, but I was also deeply scared of him at the same time.

I started to realize that I needed to come up with an escape route out of my house in case Ricky came after me again. As I was sitting in my bedroom, I started to look at all my windows to see how fast I could get the screen off. Could I get my body to fit through the window opening? I tried. Yes, I could. Thank God! I actually timed myself and jumped out of the window to see how fast I could escape, approximately twenty seconds. Knowing this gave me a deep sense of relief. However, the only thing I forgot was when I was testing the window my bedroom door was locked. So needless to say, I had to sneak around the outside of the house to get a stepstool to climb back into the window so no one would know what I was doing, especially Ricky.

As time passed, my depression grew. I felt like my family and my life were out of control. I felt lost and lonely. Ricky continually disrupted our lives. I was becoming disheartened with God, always thinking, *"Why can't you answer my prayers? Why can't he take his medicine? Why can't he understand? Why is he crazy? Why do I feel guilty for disliking him? Why do I still love him?"*

One evening in June, I sat in front of my dresser mirror in my bedroom, and I just looked at myself feeling exhausted, deeply depressed and confused. I was wondering how I could change so no one would notice me or how weak and broken-hearted I had become. How could I hide myself? I felt ugly, tired, hurt and angry. I hated life at that moment. So, I took the scissors, and I started to ravage my hair by cutting off large sections. As I was cutting, I was thinking: *"I hate the doctors! I'm mad at Ricky for ruining my family! I'm tired of being scared! I'm mad at my friends for having a better life than me! I hate mental illness! Why can't my family be normal! I hate my life!"* My hair had been down to the middle of my butt, and I cut at least fifteen inches off the first day. For the next couple of days, I continued to cut my hair out of frustration until it was less than two inches long. When it was all said and done, I had a crooked butch hair cut that looked horrible. I just wanted to be invisible — someone you wouldn't notice for any reason. I had to hide my pain and loneliness. While I was cutting, I surprisingly released some anger toward the doctors and my family for not being normal. At first, it was a relief because when I went out, no one looked at me. I blended into the crowd without anyone noticing my pain. I could hide without hiding. I think my friends were all shocked I chopped off my hair, but they never asked me why. I would have lied even if they did ask. I still did not trust anyone enough to tell them what was really going on with Ricky or how nervous and afraid I really was.

As for my family, they were shocked too. My brothers had a surprise look on their face when they noticed I had cut my hair. They didn't say anything to me but they did do a double take and shook their heads as they walked away. My mom became very concerned for my behavior. She came into my bedroom, shut the door and quietly asked, "Why are you cutting your hair?"

Putting my head down and looking at the floor, I responded, "I don't know." Feeling embarrassed.

"I know your are upset and Ricky is hard to deal with, do you want to go stay somewhere else?" She asked.

Feeling hurt and angry that she didn't want me home anymore, I snapped at her, "No! I don't want to leave! I'm fine! Just leave me alone!"

"Okay, I'm just trying to help." She said as she left my room confused and upset.

Even though her intentions were to help me, I took it the wrong way. I wanted to be home with my family to help them if they needed me. I didn't have the courage to leave and I didn't want to abandon them. The thought of it made me feel guilty.

A couple days later, my mom was in the kitchen doing dishes. Ricky came up behind her and starting poking her in the back.

"Stop it Ricky!" Mom whined, annoyed as she turned around and looked at him.

He just stood glaring at her. She turned around to finish the dishes and Ricky started to poke her harder in the back and head as he pushed her into the counter.

She yelled, "Stop it right now!" as she turned around to face him again.

Ricky said nothing as he backed up as though he was afraid of her.

Dad and Jim heard Mom yell at Ricky and they immediately ran into the kitchen.

"What wrong?" Dad asked in desperation.

"Ricky was poking me in the back and pushing me into the counter," my mom said with irritation.

"You will go into the living room," demanded Dad.

With frustration my mom said, "No, I have to finish the dishes."

Now angry himself, Jim said, "You will go now!"

My mom put the dishes down and Jim stood close to her and escorted her out of the kitchen.

"Why were you poking your mother?" asked Dad.

"I wanted to see if she's real. I don't think that is Mom!" Ricky said, looking worried.

"Stop it Rick! That is Mom. You can't keep pushing people whenever you feel like it. It has to stop!"

"You don't know what you're talking about! She is a clone!" Ricky yelled as he walked away, shaking with fear.

On June 14, 1983, we had all finished dinner. We were watching television and hanging around the house. Ricky was very agitated and as usual quarrelsome that evening. We could tell he was hallucinating again. I sat in the living room, and I heard my dad disagreeing with Ricky in the kitchen about something.

All of sudden, I heard loud commotion and a chair falling to the floor. I ran to the dining room and found Ricky trying to attack my dad! Mom, Jim and Charlie heard the commotion and ran to help, too. Ricky was swinging, trying to hit Dad in the face. Dad kept swatting Ricky's hand away and defending himself.

"Ricky! Stop!" he demanded, but Ricky continued his attack.

"No!" Ricky screamed.

"You've got horns growing out of your head! Stop it!" Ricky continued to yell as he tried to hit my dad.

"Ricky, I'm not a monster! Stop!" demanded Dad as he defended himself.

The fight moved into the dining room and got completely out of control. Ricky became more aggressive, his face muscles tightened and he was red. He screamed, "You're a monster!"

"Ricky! Stop it! Stop it!" Mom screamed.

Dad had no choice but to wrestle Ricky to the floor. As soon as my dad pinned Ricky down on the floor, Charlie and Jim jumped in to help. Dad held Ricky's neck, Jim held down his stomach, Charlie held his feet, and Mom rushed to call the Littleton Police. I stood there in shock pacing back and forth not knowing what to do.

Ricky's adrenaline was so intense and strong, my dad and two brothers had a very difficult time keeping him pinned to the floor. Ricky thrashed and kicked all over the floor and tried to get away. I stood close by watching, in tears, waiting to help if they needed me. I edged over to the front door, watching for the police.

It was terrifying to watch Ricky turn bright red with anger — his blood vessels popped out on his forehead. He screamed at everyone and flailed around completely out of control.

"Let me go! You're the devil! Let me go!" Ricky screamed with such anger and passion. "You're a communist!" he yelled, and kicked. "You're evil! Let me go!" he screamed at the top of his lungs.

The police arrived fairly quickly. I was so relieved because I feared that my dad and brothers were not going to hold Ricky down for much longer. The police handcuffed Ricky and got him to settle down. My parents explained everything, and said they needed help. Both my dad and one of the police officers talked on the phone to the doctor at the Veterans Hospital. I remember hearing the police telling the doctor that Ricky was very dangerous.

As the police were waiting to take Ricky away, Ricky kept trying to get them to arrest me. "She's a prostitute! She is from another universe! She is taking my soul away! Arrest her!" he screamed, red-faced and crazy.

"Sir, sir, just calm down," urged one of the police officers.

"You! You're black! You're a communist! You're a prostitute! You're evil! He screamed looking at me.

Arrest her!" Ricky cried with a frightening savage growl as the police officers walked him by me to the front door.

As I sat on the couch with tears in my eyes, I remember the police officer looking back at me with a gentle smile, letting me know that he didn't believe anything Ricky was saying. The police took Ricky back to the Veterans Hospital for his third admission. I was so sad for Ricky and what he believed to be true, but I was also glad that the police took him away. Maybe for a few nights we would all be able to get some sleep and not be afraid of Ricky's unexpected episodes.

Ricky had a difficult time in the hospital. He was extremely paranoid. He claimed the food and water was poisoned with copper and lead, the Japanese were after him, the Black Panthers were after him, the communists were after him, and the evil spirits were attacking his brain cells. He also believed that the hospital staff was part of the Charles Manson family. He told Mom that he could hear other patients screaming at night because he believed the staff was taking out the patients' body parts. Ricky continuously heard voices that told him not to take the medication. So he refused everything from the doctors. He became very quarrelsome with the staff. Ricky was assigned to a woman doctor, also known as, "Dr. Complete Idiot."

While Ricky was in the hospital, my parents and brother Jim decided to take a much-needed vacation to Nebraska and South Dakota. My brothers Charlie and Bruce and I decided to stay home. I was tired and didn't want to go. I just wanted some quiet time and to be left alone. It was nice to walk

L to R: Dad, Jim and Mom in Nebraska

around the house without any commotion, and I was able to sleep at night without locking my door. It was a nice break, and I know my brothers appreciated the quiet time, too.

My parents were only gone for a week. They weren't scheduled to return home until after the fourth of July. Dr. Complete Idiot called right before the fourth, asking if Ricky could come home for the weekend. I was very upset and said, "No" because the majority of the time I was home alone. I was afraid Ricky would beat me up. I called my mom in South Dakota, and she called Dr. Complete Idiot. The doctor told my mom that I should not be afraid of Ricky, and I had no reason to worry. My mom told her we had every reason to be afraid, and we didn't want him to come home! My mom had to persuade the doctor to put Ricky into a seventy-two hour mental health hold to keep him detained until my parents could get home. I guess the doctor could not take the time to look at all the paperwork and police reports to show how dangerous Ricky could be to himself and others. She must be too busy to read her files as to why he was admitted to the hospital again! He tried to beat up my dad, and she was wondering why I was afraid! My parents immediately came home, and after my mom's persuasion, the hospital did retain Ricky.

Not that it did much good — Ricky escaped from the hospital

a week later, and they did not notify my parents that he had run away. My parents found out because Ricky called my sister asking her to come pick him up on Alameda Street. My sister immediately called Mom to let her know. After my sister got a baby sitter for her children, she drove over to Alameda Street but could not find him.

Mom immediately called the hospital to find out what had happened. From what I could hear, the conversation ended with Mom calling the nurse "blockhead" as she hung up the phone — and rightly so. Calling her a blockhead was an insult to every blockhead!

We were all becoming very worried about Ricky. He had been gone for a couple of days. We assumed he was sleeping on the streets of Denver, but we didn't know where. We were afraid someone would hurt him, or he would hurt someone else. Ricky had not taken medication in a long time — and his hallucinations were bad. Who knew what he would do to a stranger? We were terrified of what could possibly happen — Ricky dying or hurting someone.

After many hours of calling the hospital, my mom finally got hold of Dr. Complete Idiot. As the conversation unfolded, Dr. Complete Idiot told her, "Leave him alone. Do not to help him if he calls."

"What? I can't do that," my mom said with anger and shock.

"Ricky has to face his illness. He needs to get help for himself," Dr. Complete Idiot stated with no concern.

"That is my child! He needs help! He is very sick!" Mom yelled through tears of frustration.

"As I said, he needs to help himself," the doctor said coldly.

My mom slammed the phone down in tears. I felt sorry for her. Here the hospital and doctor had records of Ricky's violent behaviors — and they didn't seem to care. Do they really think mentally ill people are going to admit they're mentally ill? Plus, my mom would never ignore her child. This is one of the many reasons why I'm calling this doctor a "complete idiot!" Again that's an insult to complete idiots.

Finally, three days later, Ricky called my mom to come pick him up. He was at Broadway and 16th Street in downtown Denver. She rushed downtown to retrieve him. He was tired, hungry, and dirty and he smelled. I was glad he was okay, and he didn't get hurt.

But my only thought was, what now? The next day, Mom called Dr. Complete Idiot again. "Can I please bring Ricky back to the hospital or can I get some medication from you?"

"Will Ricky come back?" the doctor asked.

At that time, Ricky realized who my mom was talking to. He grabbed the phone out of her hand and started to argue with Dr. Complete Idiot. Ricky became angry and threatening. "You people are crazy! You kill people! I'm not coming to that hospital! You're the devil. You're trying to kill me!" His voice grew louder. "I'll hurt you if you come get me! I will make them attack you!" he yelled as he threw the phone on the floor and left the room.

Mom picked up the phone and pleaded, "Please help. Ricky is getting violent again."

Dr. Complete Idiot hung up and immediately called the Littleton Police for her, the only thing she did do right.

The Littleton Police showed up quickly. It was a good thing they did because Ricky was threatening Mom again. "It's your fault! If I have to go back to the hospital, I will have the demons get you! You will go to hell!"

"Please, Ricky, I'm only trying to help you," my mom cried.

"Aliens told me that you're bad! You're evil!" he screamed at her. "I'm sick because of you! You told the demons to make me sick! You told them to possess me! I hate you!" He continued his mad rant.

Watching my mom's pain on her face, I knew it hurt her feelings because she was so dedicated to helping Ricky. It was hard for her to put those feelings aside and know that it was only his illness talking. He was becoming more violent — and you never knew what would trigger a violent outburst.

While Ricky was arguing with mom, I snuck out of the house and waited for the police. Luckily, one of the police officers was familiar with Ricky. I showed one police officer to the back door and while they other came through the front door, because they were afraid Ricky would try to run as soon as he saw them. They caught Ricky off guard and were able to handcuff and arrest him.

As Ricky stood by the police car, he was calling my mom bad names. "Bitch! Pig! I hate you! You're a horrible mom! You're evil!"

As I watched out of the window, tears were rolling down her cheeks as she stood there. Needless to say, some of the neighbors were outside watching, and my mom became very embarrassed. Ricky would not stop yelling names at her.

The police officer who had been to our house before asked my mom, "How could this happen?"

"I don't know. We can't get help," Mom said, the desperation changing in her voice.

"We will get him some help. We will make sure he gets into the hospital," the officer offered with strong assurance.

The police officer realized we lacked support in dealing with Ricky. I think it made my mom feel better knowing that someone else recognized the issue. The police took Ricky back to the Veterans Hospital.

The situation with Ricky was not getting better when he returned to the hospital. It was now the middle of July '83, and he continued to refuse medication. He also threatened to kill the therapist and other staff members. My mom went to visit him and to meet with Dr. Complete Idiot. Ricky was very irritable and angry with Mom. He blamed her for his being admitted to the hospital.

The doctor, Mom, Ricky, and another male attendant were in a room, discussing medications with Ricky, when all of sudden, he stood up, grabbed an eraser, and threw it at my mom's face.

Mom screamed as she jumped back from the table.

The attendant rushed to Ricky's side and grabbed him.

"It's your fault I'm here! You're a terrible mom! You're going to pay for this!" Ricky yelled at Mom. The attendant directed Ricky out of the room.

Dr. Complete Idiot stated to my mom, "I think it's best you go, Mrs. Nau."

Mom sat there in shock as the doctor left the room. They never finished the conversation on how to help Ricky or what medication they needed to get him to take. Mom left confused.

The eraser didn't injure her but her feelings were badly hurt. Over these last couple of years, Ricky had never been violent toward Mom, but during the last few weeks his anger seemed to focus on her.

Finally, the doctor decided to proceed with getting a court order against Ricky to force medication. A week later, they were in court in front of a judge. The hospital tried to convince the judge that Ricky needed forced medication. Ricky fought back and explained to the judge in a very intelligent way that the medication caused bad side effects — and that he believed he did not need it. I don't know what in the world happened, but Ricky won! I guess the hospital was not prepared for Ricky to speak so sanely and intelligently. The judge felt that the way the doctors wanted to force the medication was not appropriate. The hospital wanted to give to shots in Ricky's stomach, which can be a very painful procedure.

What is most frustrating to my family was the fact that neither the doctor nor the hospital staff ever took the time to inform my family that they were going to court until after the fact. If my family had been involved, maybe we could have explained to the judge about all that was happening at home and how out of control Ricky was becoming. My family members never got that chance to defend themselves, ensure their safety, or explain why Ricky urgently needed help.

For the next couple of weeks, Ricky continued to refuse medication. The hospital had to help him because he was a veteran. However, I don't think they really cared about him, since they could not force him to take medication. I'm pretty sure the hospital and the doctor did not want Ricky as a patient anymore.

I know the hospital talked to him about going into long-term hospital care or doing some type of vocational rehabilitation. I guess I have a hard time understanding why the hospital would give Ricky a choice, first of all. Second, what in the world would make them think a mentally ill person has the ability to make a sound decision? Ricky needed to be in the hospital — and he desperately needed medication. I don't understand why the hospital did not go back to court and fight again — and this time include our family so the judge could understand very clearly how sick Ricky was and how violent he was becoming. I believe in my heart that the judge did not understand the complete picture. I think he would have made a different decision if he knew the truth about what was happening at home. Unfortunately, Dr. Complete Idiot didn't think we needed to be involved.

Ricky made the decision to enter vocational rehabilitation. I was dumbfounded. How do you rehabilitate a mentally ill person who does not take medication, believes he does not need to take medication, and does not believe he is sick in the first place? This whole concept sounded ridiculous for Ricky. I figured it was just a way for the hospital to push him out of its care because it did not want to take responsibility for him. I still feel very angry at the hospital and its lack of productive care. Ricky's therapist set up a vocational rehabilitation appointment for August 23. I thought, *"Now this should be interesting..."*

My mom always stayed in contact with the hospital, therapist and doctor to encourage care for Ricky. Both Mom and Dad were dedicated in visiting Ricky at the hospital and letting him know that he always had family support. I didn't go visit Ricky at the hospital this time — I could not handle the emotional aspect of it anymore. I was getting to the point where I shoved the whole problem to the back of my mind and acted like Ricky's problem did not exist.

School would be starting in a few weeks, and I was going to be a senior. I looked forward to my last year of high school, and I prayed every night that this year would be better than the last two years. I really wanted to enjoy school and my friends, even though I felt like I had a dark cloud over my head that was about to erupt into a vicious storm!

At the beginning of August '83, I had to go get my senior pictures taken for the yearbook. Obviously, I wasn't too excited about this. I had chopped off my hair; I looked ugly; I felt insecure; I wasn't happy; and most importantly, I didn't feel like smiling! The photographer kept trying to joke with me to get me to laugh. I did a few times and

My Senior Picture

probably got some okay pictures.

I remember him having the camera very close to my face and stating, "Your eyes remind me of an old soul." He then asked, "Why are they so sad?"

I almost burst into tears. I wanted so badly to tell this strange man that I had a mentally ill brother who I was afraid was going to hurt my family and that I wanted him to be locked up. Of course, I kept my mouth shut and just played dumb. "I'm not sad," I said with a crooked smile. "Are we done? Can I go now?"

He looked at me weird, but said we had enough pictures. He knew I was lying and just wanted to get out of there. I'm glad he let me go without any more questions.

Days later on August 10th, either Dr. Complete Idiot or one of Ricky's therapists decided to let him have more privileges at the hospital. They decided that he could go outside and attend a volleyball activity. As his group was walking to the volleyball area, Ricky ran away.

Dr. Complete Idiot called my mom to warn her, "Ricky ran away from the hospital, and he will probably be coming home."

"What?" Mom was slack jawed. "How did he leave the hospital?"

"He ran away from a volleyball activity," the doctor said.

"Why was he outside?" Mom asked, baffled. "You knew he was a risk."

Dr. Complete Idiot did not answer the question. She only stated, "We will only hold his bed for twenty-four hours."

Her frustration at the boiling point, Mom asked, "Are you going to get him? He was in your care!"

"No, we will not come and get him," the doctor flatly replied, with no concern or guilt.

That night the police came by around dinnertime to see if everything was okay. I'm not sure how, but the police knew Ricky had run away from the hospital. Maybe the doctor called them again, we don't know.

If Dr. Complete Idiot did call the police, wouldn't that be a red flag stating that she knew Ricky was dangerous? But yet, she would only hold his bed for twenty-four hours. If he was dangerous, why wouldn't the hospital do everything in its power to get him off the streets before he hurt himself or someone else?

The police were nice — and they wanted to make sure that Ricky was not causing any problems. It felt great to know that the police (or anyone) knew Ricky was in bad shape — and that they cared enough to check up on us. It made me feel more comfortable about the situation because I was very scared that Ricky could show up at anytime — and we had no idea what state of mind he would be in. Watching my parents' reaction to the police, I think they felt the same. They knew that the police were there if we needed them.

Ricky did show up later that night. He was acting bizarre, as usual, but at least he was not angry or violent. He was actually very quiet and kept to himself. Since the beginning of June, when Ricky was home, he had slept in the backyard because he worried about the devils in his bedroom. This particular evening, very late, I got up and looked out my bedroom window to see if he was sleeping outside. First, I wanted to make sure he was out there and not inside the house. Second, I felt so bad for him. I just stared and watched him sleep and wondered, *"why him?"* I also thought about what I would do if he tried to hurt my family or me. How would I respond? For some reason, I felt like I needed to start preparing. I got lost in my thoughts and fears, and I probably sat at my window for hours, just watching and thinking, *"what do I do...?"*

The next morning, Mom called Dr. Complete Idiot, telling her that Ricky had come home and asking if she could get some medication to put in Ricky's orange juice. The doctor said, "No."

She also told my mom, "Don't bother bringing Ricky back to the hospital. We gave up his bed to someone else."

Mom gasped with disbelief, "What? It's barely been twenty-four hours. How could you give up his bed so fast?"

Dr. Complete Idiot said, "There are no reasons for him to be here since we cannot give him medication."

"Why can't you do an court appeal?" my mom asked in confusion.

"No, we can't do that," said the doctor abruptly and rudely.

"Why? I don't understand! It makes no sense to me. Is there someone else I could talk to? Is there another hospital I can go to? What else can I do?" Mom pleaded.

"I suggest you kick Ricky out of the house until he is ready to accept his illness," stated the dumb doctor.

"I can't do that, he needs us!" Mom said, her voice rising in distress.

"Sorry, Mrs. Nau, I need to go."

And with that, the doctor hung up. She had basically blew Mom off and didn't offer any help or advice. The doctor decided to completely give up on Ricky. She did not believe that he was worth the time and effort to help. A young man, twenty-two year old was not worth it in her book! I was seething! Did she really think a mother would give up on her own child? How sad to hear this doctor imply she did not think this human being was worthy of help.

For the next week and a half, Ricky did okay. The family, as usual was tense and worried. We had learned to be very careful about what we said to him to make sure we did not trigger any violent episodes. He would consistently say weird things to us, and we could always tell when he heard voices, but we learned to ignore it and go on with our day. Ricky still occasionally poked us to see if we were real or swiped his hand over the top of our heads to brush away the evil spirits or insects that he saw. I personally tried to avoid him as much as possible always finding a reason to go to my friend's house or to go sit at a park. I would go anywhere to get away from the house and the fear.

Ricky was starting to become more paranoid of the outside world. When the phone rang, he would think it was a call from Japan, and the evil spirits were tracking him down. He didn't want anyone to answer the phone because he felt our phone was tapped. We had to reassure him that it was just our friends calling. Ricky continuously thought that the neighbors were communists, rallying up an attack against him. He would not go near the front door or look out the front window in fear that the neighbors would see him and send evil spirits or poisonous air his way.

On August 23, Ricky had his appointment with the vocational rehabilitation counselor at the VA Federal Center in Lakewood. My mom was able to talk Ricky into keeping his appointment. She was sick with a bad case of the flu, and really did not want to go, but she didn't want to give up him either. She was praying and hoping that this counselor could help him in some way.

As they drove to the appointment, Ricky wanted to argue with her. He thought my mom was taking him to the Veterans Hospital, but she had to keep telling him she was going the opposite direction. Once they arrived to the appointment, Ricky spoke with the counselor, but my mom was not allowed to be included in the meeting. Ricky met with the counselor for only a few minutes. Basically, the only thing that the counselor said to Ricky was that he qualified for so many hours of education that the VA would pay for whenever he was ready. I didn't know if this counselor had any idea that he was mentally ill. My mom never even got an opportunity to talk to the counselor.

After the meeting, while they were driving home, Ricky became agitated again and started yelling at Mom.

"I know you're a communist and you're the devil in disguise! That's why you made me come to this meeting!"

"No, Rick, I am not the devil nor am I a communist. You are the one who made this meeting with the doctor. Don't you remember?" Mom said quietly.

Ricky sat there for a moment, and then Mom could see out of the corner of her eye that Ricky was staring and looking at something strange above her head.

Ricky then hit her very hard in the arm while she was driving.

Mom, very upset, said, "What are you doing? Why did you do that?" She tried to slow the car down.

"Your head is turning into an insect! Stop it! Why are you doing that?" Ricky yelled at her.

Ricky started to freak out and got scared. He rolled down the car window and tried to climb out while the car was moving around forty-five miles per hour. Mom immediately pulled over to the side of the road and almost caused an accident.

She was desperately trying to keep Ricky in the car by pulling his arm and shirt, yelling, "I'm stopping the car! Please, Rick! Stay in the car!"

"I want out!" he cried.

"It's okay, Rick! I promise you, I'm not an insect. Please stay in the car! Don't be scared!" She frantically pleaded, "Please, Rick, it's a hallucination."

He finally stopped trying to climb out the window. She sat there quietly for a moment on the side of the road, catching her thoughts. "Ricky, you have to believe me. I'm not a monster or an insect. I would never hurt you. Let's just go home. It's okay." Ricky sat there staring at her in fear. "Rick, I'm not going to hurt you. Will you stay in the car if I start driving home?" Mom asked gently.

Rick nodded, "yes."

It was very hard for my mom to drive the rest of the way home because Ricky was very distracting. He continuously swiped his hand above her head.

By the time they got home, Ricky was very agitated and angry again. Within a few minutes, he frantically paced around the house looking for his car keys, quickly packed his things, got his money, got into his car, and drove away. We tried to stop him, but it happened so quickly, we couldn't. Not expecting him to run away from the house and drive his car since he was so paranoid about society, we had no idea where he was going.

Four days passed, and we still had not heard anything from him. We were all very upset and worried that he had gotten into a car accident or that he had attacked someone. My mom called the state patrol a couple times a day to see if he was involved in any accidents. Secretly I was hoping he would not come home. I was tired of living in fear of him. Though I didn't want him to get hurt, I just didn't want him home anymore. Of course, I started to feel guilty for thinking that way. So, when we finally did hear from him, I was relieved to hear that he was okay.

Ricky was stranded in Glenwood Springs, Colorado. His car had broken down in Wyoming, and he lost his wallet. He had a few dollars in his pocket so he was able take a bus from Wyoming to Glenwood Springs.

My brother Jim had just gotten home from his visit to South Dakota. He rented a tow bar so he could tow Ricky's car home. Jim went and picked up Ricky in Glenwood Springs, and then they drove to Wyoming to get his car. From what Jim told me, Ricky kept arguing with him the whole time and thought everyone was out to get him. Ricky was becoming extremely paranoid by this time. Jim had a hard time keeping him calm during those few days. The only thing that Jim could do to keep him calm was to continually agree with him that everyone was after him and that the voices were correct. If Jim did not agree, Ricky would have turned on him and either run away or attacked him. Jim did not want that to happen. He was walking a very fine line with him, and he did whatever he needed to do to get him home safely. Luckily, the motel in Wyoming found Ricky's wallet and mailed it home.

During this time, school started — and it was the beginning of my senior year. I was excited and glad to be back in school and started cheering again for football and soccer games. Again school had become a safe haven for me. I was glad to have a place to go where I felt safe from Ricky. The only problem was, during the day I was constantly worried about my mom and brothers who were at home. I had a hard time studying and concentrating because I felt so uptight about Ricky — and whether if anyone at home needed my help. I actually started to get anxiety attacks from the stress. During these attacks, I could not catch my breath; it felt like an asthma attack, like I was suffocating.

By this time, I absolutely would not allow any of my friends to come over to my house. My mom was good about letting me use the car. She knew I was too afraid to have my friends over because who knew what Ricky would say or do. He was starting to talk more about outer space and aliens. He was also very quarrelsome — and if you walked by him, he would push you. If you looked at him, he would push you. If you spoke to him, he would push you. It was definitely intense — and tension was building up like air being forced into a full balloon.

I found out my brother Gene was coming home from Tennessee for a visit the first week of September '83. I was so relieved and happy to hear that. I think my brother wanted to see if he could help Ricky, plus, I think he wanted to see Jim. They had not seen each other in many years. My mom had stayed in contact with Gene and kept him filled in on all the problems; however, Gene had not been home in years, so he had not seen how sick Ricky was in person. I was glad he would finally see with his own eyes how bad the situation had become.

My brother Gene is a quiet man, but when he speaks he does so with eloquence in a soothing, gentle voice. The way he talks makes you want to listen. I was hoping that his gentleness would rub off on Ricky, and that Gene would be able to talk him into taking medication. Plus, it also made me feel better to know we would have another male around the house, just in case Ricky had another violent episode. In a weird way, it made me feel better to know we had power in numbers: five males (Dad, Jim, Gene, Charlie and Bruce) and then Mom and me. Ricky wouldn't be able to stand up to five males; at least you wouldn't think so. I was thrilled that Gene was coming home.

CHAPTER SEVEN

Nightmare About to Begin

O n a beautiful September day, Gene arrived home. It was so nice to see him again and catch up on all that was going on in his life. He had just received his Masters of Science, and now he was starting to work on his Ph.D. in cellular molecular biology in Tennessee. I was so proud of him - what an accomplishment! The family was relieved to have him home, and Jim was excited to see and spend some time with him, since it had been many years. Having Gene home also put me in a better mood and made me feel more secure.

September is one of my favorite months because the sun is shining, and the weather is still warm. You can smell and feel fall right around the corner. The leaves on the trees are just starting to change color and it makes me feel warm inside. I absolutely love the change of seasons and all the vibrant yellow, red and orange fall colors. It's also football season, and I was busy cheering at all the football and soccer games. It was always fun when we played other high schools within the Littleton area, because I got to see a lot of old friends. It was nice to be busy with school and cheering so I didn't have to be home so much.

Homecoming was in three weeks, and we started to prepare for the parade and all the games. I felt glad to have something to look forward to.

Ricky had been calm since Gene got home. Just as I thought, Gene provided a sense of ease around the house and with him. Ricky trusted Gene and tended to follow and copy him. Gene believed strongly in natural remedies. He encouraged Ricky to try the vitamin program again that he'd received when he went to the Bio-Brain Center in New Jersey. Gene took great care of his body and took vitamins, so when Ricky watched Gene take his vitamins, it encouraged him to take vitamins too. Ricky did seem to be in better spirits, however, he was still sleeping outside in the backyard. Occasionally, I would see him walking around in the backyard, grabbing "fictitious things" in midair as if they were really there. He would still make paranoid comments about people walking or driving by the house. He believed they were all after him, and he would also hallucinate seeing them turn into insects or monsters. Even though he was still difficult — and we still had to be very careful about what we said — there was a little more sense of peace around the house with Gene home.

Gene and Jim decided to take Ricky camping down to Buena Vista, Colorado. They went for a few days to do some hiking and exploring on Mt. Antero. Ricky was excited to get into the mountains; it gave him sense of calmness like no other place could.

He really needed to get away from the house and get some fresh air. The family needed him to go away too, just to get a break.

I was worried about Gene and Jim taking Ricky camping. I was not sure how Ricky would

Mt. Antero (14,269 feet)
Buena Vista, CO

112

respond. I was afraid he would freak out and run away or attack one of them. Even though they were gone, I still could not sleep at night, just from worrying about them.

After they got home, Gene and Jim told me that everything had gone pretty well. Overall, Ricky seemed to act somewhat normal, and he would only occasionally say weird things here and there.

Jim and Gene had not seen each, so they had a lot of catching up to do. One evening while they were sitting by the fire, Jim told Gene about his horrible experiences in Vietnam. Jim had never spoken to anyone about it until that night. It was a very intense conversation between the two of them. Jim was finally releasing his terrible memories and Gene was intently listening.

Ricky must have felt left out of the conversation because out of the blue, he interrupted and said loudly, "Do you know I have higher consciousness than Jesus? God thinks my brain is unique, the most developed brain on the planet."

"Yeah, Rick, you're right. Everyone has a unique brain and everyone is special in his own way. You're the only one who has a brain exactly like yours," Gene said in a gentle voice. He did not want to get Ricky caught up in his unreal world, so he felt it was important to acknowledge him and make him feel included.

With a quirky smile Jim stated, "Yeah, right, who would want a brain like yours?"

They all started to laugh, including Ricky. The joke seemed to release some tension, and Ricky sat quietly the rest of the night listening to Jim's Vietnam stories.

The next day, they decided to climb a 14,000-foot Mt. Antero. When they reached three-fourths of the way up, Ricky had a burst of energy and ran up the rest of the way, which is really difficult to do with lower levels of oxygen.

"Ricky, slow down and wait for us!" Gene yelled up to him.

"Ah, let him have his win," Jim said.

In the distance, Gene and Jim watched Ricky summit the top of the mountain. When Ricky reached the top, he jumped up and down, spinning around with his arms in the air yelling, "I won! I won!"

"It's good to see Ricky acting like his old self again," Gene commented to Jim as they both laughed.

When Gene and Jim reached the top they noticed how beautiful it was that day. The September air was very clear and calm. The sun was shining, the sky was a deep blue, and the trees were starting to turn colors in the distance. It was a very beautiful and peaceful day, and they were the only people on top of the mountain.

They all stood quietly, a few feet apart from each other, admiring the splendor all around them. They felt a sense of deep peace in their own way. Jim felt peace from the trauma of Vietnam. Gene felt peace from working extremely long hours in grad school, and Ricky felt a peace of mind — a sense of normalcy.

From what Gene told me, it was a very special moment for all of them, something he would never forget.

As for the rest of the camping trip, the only thing that really bothered Gene was Ricky's abnormal breathing patterns while he slept. Ricky would breath very heavily and very erratically. Gene said it sounded like a bear. Ricky was sleeping twenty-five feet away and his breathing woke Gene up. Gene was not sure if this was part of his illness, but it did cause him concern.

Ricky also informed them during their camping trip that he had a thing against salt. He would not tolerate it on his food because he thought it would allow the devil into his body. From my understanding, whenever Ricky brought up odd comments like this, Jim and Gene were able to diffuse Ricky's thought patterns before he got too weird.

I'm just grateful they all got home safely.

But then things started to take a turn for the worse. The first two weeks of September were the calm before the storm. Ricky stopped taking his vitamins and still would not take any medication. He started to get agitated again. If my brothers or I would walk by him, he would not hesitate to, as usual, to push us or swipe the top of our heads as if we had demons above us. I did everything I could to avoid him.

One evening my mom, Bruce and I were watching the late night news. Ricky came into the room very upset, insisting he knew where Beth Miller was located. Beth Miller was the young girl who had been abducted from Idaho Springs, Colorado a few weeks earlier, and it was on all the news stations. Unfortunately, she was never found, God rest her soul.

Ricky was so intent on finding Beth Miller, he yelled, "I have to find her!" as he ran around the house to look for Jim's car keys because he was going to take off to go to Fairplay, Colorado to go find Beth Miller in a mine.

Ricky ran to the phone and called the Idaho Springs Police Department and told them, "I know where Beth Miller is! She is in a mine, and the evil spirits or aliens have taken her." The police hung up on Ricky, which made him more upset.

By this time, it was close to 10:30 p.m., and Mom and I were scared of Ricky driving erratically up into the mountains in the middle of the dark night. We were afraid he would cause an accident or fall into a mine not knowing where he was located.

"Please Rick, the police will find her. It's too dark; you can't go to the mountains at this time of night. Please Rick, stay home, and we will call the police again tomorrow," said my mom as she frantically tried to calm Ricky down before he took off.

With a worried look, Mom told Bruce, "Lock the front door."

Bruce did what she told him. He stood by the front door prepared to physically stop Ricky from trying to get out. He started hitting and pushing Bruce. Ricky was very determined. "Let me out!" he demanded. "I need to find Beth!"

"No, you're not!" Bruce yelled back.

Bruce had to wrestle Ricky up against the wall. Meanwhile, Mom and I jumped in to help stop Ricky from fighting with Bruce. I kept grabbing Ricky's arms to prevent him from hitting Bruce and my mom kept trying to calm him down. "Rick, please stop. We will find Beth tomorrow. It's too late right now. Calm down, she will be okay."

My brother Gene heard the commotion from downstairs and ran upstairs to help Bruce get control of Ricky. Eventually, my mom and Gene were able to calm Ricky down. They manipulated him into thinking that he could call the police the next day to tell them where Beth Miller was located, so they could go find her.

By the next morning, Ricky's thought process and attention moved on to other issues for the day.

After that evening, Ricky kept deteriorating. He was continually disturbed and angry. He constantly started fights with Jim, Bruce, Charlie or me. When anyone walked by him, he yelled, pushed, slapped or punched them with much more anger and intensity. He would do whatever he could to start a fight. It was getting to be too much for everyone. Tension built up to such a level that no one felt comfortable or at ease.

We could no longer carry on any normal type of conversation with Ricky. "How are you today?" someone would ask. Ricky would just blankly stare as if any of us were complete strangers, and he did not know us.

"Are you okay, Rick, do you need anything?" I asked. He would just look at me like I was crazy for talking to him.

He also continuously talked to the voices in his head, telling the demons or monsters or aliens to leave him alone. At nighttime, he started to walk around the backyard yelling at the moon, "I know the demons are here! I am the higher being. You are not going to crucify me! Stop taking my soul! The aliens will get you! I know the demons live here! Leave me alone!"

Ricky's physical appearance deteriorated again — his skin had become pasty white. His eyes were sunken with dark circles. He was thin and had an aura around him that was completely negative. Sometimes, he walked by and the hairs on the back of my neck stood up. I felt such a deep sense of fear in my bones, and I had a terrible feeling in my heart that something bad was going to happen. I felt so much anxiety; I was physically feeling drained and sick. I was having a hard time sleeping and focusing on my schoolwork.

By this time it was Monday, September 19th. I had cheer practice after school and had to prepare for homecoming the following week. My squad started to get on my case about my attitude.

"What's wrong with you, Debbie? You're being cold. You're distant. You won't talk to us anymore. You seem to be mad at us all of the time. What's the problem?" they all asked - in separate questions, of course.

At first I was shocked and felt attacked. I snapped angrily as I walked away, "Nothing is wrong!"

But they knew something was wrong. By the end of practice, I could not hold it in anymore, I fell to the ground and broke down into tears. All my fears came rushing out uncontrollably, "I'm scared to death to be home! I'm afraid something bad is going to happen to my family!" I cried.

"What is going on, Debbie? What are you talking about?" one of the girls asked.

"I can't sleep at night; I always have to lock my doors!" I cried some more.

Confused, my friend asked, "Why do you have to lock your doors?"

"I can't be alone with Ricky! I'm afraid to go home," I tearfully admitted as I broke down into hysterical tears, losing all sense of control.

My friends did not understand what was going on because I was not adequately explaining things. I was just crying out statements. They all looked at me confused.

"Do you want to come stay at my house?" one girlfriend offered.

"I can't! I have to be home," I cried with frustration. I wanted so badly to escape, but I just could not leave my family. I knew I needed to be there in case something happened. I finally got up and told them I had to leave.

Gene had to leave on Wednesday, September 21st. He had to get back to school. I was extremely sad to see him go; it was a nice and comfortable feeling having him home. I was also very jealous of him leaving because he had a reason to escape this bad environment. I remember when I said goodbye to him, I had this weird thought in my mind to say to him, *Take a good look at our faces because it might be the last time you see us.* I never said the words aloud because I didn't want to sound paranoid. However, I couldn't shake this terrible feeling, and I was starting to have bad dreams. I felt like God was warning me. In actuality... He was.

The next day, Ricky kept calling the Navy to try to re-enlist. He kept telling them that the spirits told him to go back to the Navy. I can't remember how many calls he made, but it was a lot. I was starting to wonder if the Navy was going to send the police to our house. I was actually hoping they would, so they would arrest him and take him to the hospital. Unfortunately, no one showed up.

During this time, my mom continuously called doctors in the yellow pages to try to get help or medicine for Ricky. The problem was they would never prescribe medication unless they saw him in person. Well, trying to get Ricky into a car to go to the doctor was impossible. He would run away if you even mentioned driving to the doctor. It was hopeless to get him to the doctor and get help. God bless my mom's heart, she never stopped trying.

It was now Friday, September 23rd, Ricky's angry spurts were starting to last longer and longer. Ricky would purposely come into the room just to start a fight. All of us kids tried to be patient and understanding, but it was hard.

Unfortunately for Bruce, he walked by Ricky and must have looked at him wrong because Ricky lost his temper and punched Bruce really hard in the stomach again! Poor Bruce. He kept his cool, didn't say anything, and backed away with anger in his eyes. Mom was concerned for Bruce and wanted to take him to the doctor to get checked. He had just gotten out of the hospital for viral meningitis. He was weak and not feeling well, but Bruce would not go to the doctor. He just wanted to be left alone and away from Ricky.

The next day, Saturday morning, I was trying to relax in the living room, watching cartoons. Mom and my brother Jim were in the kitchen eating.

Ricky kept pacing around the house. He was very upset and seemed to be in a trance-like state. He would stand for minutes at a time contemplating the wall, rocking back and forth. We could tell he was listening to the voices in his head. He went into the kitchen to sit at the table. Jim sat on one end of the table with his back up to the wall while Ricky sat at the other end.

Ricky was speaking erratically. "The spaceship is coming to get me! They are telling me that I am a higher being. The demons are living in your ears. I don't believe you're real! Your face keeps changing!" he snarled while focusing intently on Jim.

"Oh, Rick," Jim said.

Ricky got so mad he grabbed his spoon and threw it as hard as he could at Jim's face.

Ricky immediately jumped up enraged and lunged toward Jim with both hands, screaming, "I'm going to kill you!"

Jim quickly jumped up to protect himself. Unfortunately, he was backed up against the wall and had a hard time getting out from behind the table.

"Stop it, Rick!" Jim yelled as Mom yelled at the same time, "Stop it! Stop it!"

Ricky started punching Jim in the face. Jim's glasses flew off his face so he had a hard time seeing Ricky. Jim tried desperately to hold him back and not once did he hit him.

Ricky just kept punching him in the face. My mom screamed with tears rolling down her face, "Help! Help!" as she tried to stop him.

I immediately jumped up and ran into the dining room. Charlie and Bruce ran up from downstairs and my dad ran out of the bathroom. By this time, the fight had moved into the dining room, and Ricky had gotten Jim onto the floor, punching him.

"Stop it, Rick! Stop it!" we were all screaming.

Adrenaline pumped through Ricky making him even stronger. I got scared and started to cry not knowing what to do. Ricky was out of control! My mom rushed to the phone to call the police.

It took Dad, Charlie and Bruce to pull Ricky off Jim and then wrestle him to the floor. My dad had to actually sit on top of Ricky. Charlie held his feet. Bruce held his arms. Once Jim got up and got a clear head, he too, helped my dad hold Ricky down.

Ricky's screams were un-earthly, almost like an animal being killed, "Get off me! I hate you! Let me go! I'm going to kill you! Get off me!"

I paced in front of the door waiting for the police. The police, now familiar with us came immediately. As they entered the house, Ricky was still screaming with a bright red face, "Get off me!"

The officer handcuffed Ricky as everyone held him to the floor. With a quiet, soothing, monotone voice, the police officer spoke to Ricky, "Sir, if you don't settle down, these handcuffs will be painful. Sir, you need to calm down or we will have no choice but to get rough. Sir, I know you are upset. Please calm down so we can help you."

By this time, Ricky's struggles ceased and he started to breathe and calm down.

Once again, my parents had to explain everything that was happening. The police decided to take Ricky to the Littleton Police Station.

I felt sorry for Jim because he was hurt. He had a bruise cheek and scratch by his eye and was visibly shaken. Jim felt horrible for Ricky, feeling bad that he'd caused Ricky to get upset. Jim kept pacing the house, disturbed by what had happened. He had a hard time walking around the house because he could not see. His glasses had been knocked off when Ricky was hitting him, and now we could not find them.

It was hard on all of us to see Ricky so upset and out of control. It had finally come to the point that it was impossible to predict what he was going to say or do.

At the police station, the police called the Veterans Hospital to admit Ricky but the hospital would not take him. The police told the hospital that Ricky was dangerous. They got no response. The police then took Ricky to Arapahoe Mental Health located in Littleton. My mom and dad were in contact with the police the whole time. Mom also talked to Arapahoe Mental Health about trying to get Ricky some help. She asked them to get Ricky admitted to the Veterans Hospital. They said they could not do that and the hospital was full, but we know from the police that the hospital did not want to take him back. So she made some other phone calls for help. Nothing. Mom then called Arapahoe Mental Health again to find out that the police were already in the process of taking Ricky down to the State Hospital located in Pueblo, Colorado.

I could not stop thinking about my sick brother. I kept praying to God that the doctors would see how sick he really was and admit him. After this incident, I could not sleep and my hands would not stop trembling. I almost felt like I was going to have another anxiety attack.

The next day, Sunday, my mom called the State Hospital to find out which doctor was handling Ricky's case. She wanted to have an opportunity to speak with him about Ricky's behavior. Unfortunately, he was not there. Due to the circumstances, there is no name I can give this doctor other than "Dr. Dumb-Ass" because he suffers from a severe case of the "Rectal Cranial Inversion" Syndrome. The hospital told my mom to call back on Monday at 4:00 p.m. to speak to Dr. Dumb-Ass. The nurses also told her that Ricky was having a hard time adjusting to the hospital. He would walk the halls all night long because he could not sleep in his room. Ricky thought his roommate was putting out fumes from his mouth, which contained ammonia gas, and he believed he could not breathe because of it.

My brother Jim called Dr. Dumb-Ass Monday afternoon around 4:00 p.m. because Mom had to be at work. Jim told my parents that the doctor had not yet seen Ricky. He felt that the doctor did not seem like he knew what he was talking about or had any concept about what to do. Jim tried to explain the situation about Ricky but Dr. Dumb-Ass would not listen. Jim was very frustrated and upset over the conversation. He knew immediately that this doctor had no experience in dealing with an acute schizophrenic like Ricky.

On Tuesday morning, September 27th (which is also my brother Jeff's birthday), Mom was able to call and talk to Dr. Dumb-Ass. The doctor told her, "I don't think anything is wrong with Ricky. I personally don't understand why he was brought down here."

"What! Are you kidding me?" Mom asked, incredulous with shock.

"The police brought him down because he violently attacked his brother," Mom explained angrily.

With frustration, my mom continued to describe the difficult situations with Ricky and all his prior history of seeing hallucinations, hearing voices, refusing to eat, acting violent, and seeing the devil.

Once again, Dr. Dumb-Ass told her, "I don't think Ricky is sick."

I think she nearly fell off her seat. How could this doctor be so dumb? "How could you say that? Did you not hear me? Did you not check his history with the doctors at the Veterans Hospital?" she asked as she almost completely lost it.

"Oh, well, it's too late. I already released him from the hospital," he said nonchalantly.

"You idiot!" Mom yelled with tears in her eyes and slammed down the phone.

Hours later, Mom found out that they had sent Ricky to the Santa Fe House, in Littleton (part of Arapahoe Mental Health). Later we also discovered that Dr. Dumb-Ass only interviewed Ricky for approximately fifteen minutes. He did not check police reports or hospital records, nor did he speak to any other doctors.

He just let him go because he had no clue how to be a psychiatrist.

I was so upset I went into my room, and started crying and hitting my pillow out of frustration. Thinking, *"I don't want Ricky to coming back home. Why can't anyone help us! I hate doctors!"*

Later that day, Ricky called my mom from the Santa Fe House and asked if he could come home to shower and get clean clothes. With deep fear and hesitation, Mom went and picked him up and brought him home.

I was terrified to know that Ricky was coming back home. Everyone living in that house was absolutely on edge, driven by fear mixed with love and a real desire to help — but fear pushed everyone's emotions and created tension. When my mom got home with him, she called the Santa Fe House to talk to the head counselor, who unfortunately, was an idiot, too. He did not want to deal with Ricky, so he assigned him to another counselor. My mom continued to ask this man if she could get some medication for Ricky or a psychiatrist's name she could call. He didn't offer any help and didn't seem to really care.

That evening, my mom told Ricky that he would have to go back to the Santa Fe House the next day because he could no longer live at our house. He didn't say much — he just sat at the picnic table in the backyard and stared. For a moment, he did yell at Bruce for looking at him, but Bruce immediately backed away and left the house to avoid any problems.

Ricky was tired and quiet. He just slept in the backyard all night and stayed to himself, while the rest of us kept our bedroom doors locked and barely slept.

I left for school the next morning, Wednesday, September 28. I was worried about leaving Mom home with my troubled brother. I really didn't want to go to school. Even though my brothers Jim, Bruce and Charlie were home, I felt very uneasy. Ricky had no control of his mind from one minute to the next, and I knew he could explode at any time. I felt sick to my stomach and very light-headed, but I also knew that going to school was an escape. So I left. I was nervous all day and had quite a few friends ask me, "What's wrong?" I said nothing. How do you explain a feeling of fear and sickness all bunched up together? I just kept quiet and tried to avoid talking to anyone.

My mom got Ricky to go back down to the Santa Fe House later that day to talk to their assigned counselor. When they arrived, their assigned counselor was on the phone. They waited and waited but she would not get off the phone. My mom was very frustrated because Ricky was getting nervous and uptight. He didn't want to be there, and he kept pacing back and forth in the waiting room — all Mom ever wanted was to get some help for my brother, so she could protect the rest of her family.

Finally, an older man, whom we will call "Mr. Bonehead," came into the room and talked to Mom. She explained the situation with Ricky and asked if they could help her find a home or a place for him to get some medical attention.

Mr. Bonehead said, "We do not have anything for Ricky."

Mom told Mr. Bonehead, "The State Hospital told me that the Santa Fe House had resources to help him find a halfway house. That is why the hospital sent him down here yesterday."

Mr. Bonehead acted like he had no clue as to what my mom was talking about. "I don't have any place for Ricky. I don't know why the hospital said that."

Mr. Bonehead then turned to Ricky and said, "Why don't you come with me into another room to talk? Mrs. Nau, you can stay here. We will be right back."

I don't understand why he felt it was necessary to exclude my mom. When they came back, Mr. Bonehead told Mom, "Ricky has declined our treatment plan."

"What treatment plan?" Mom asked, confused. Mr. Bonehead did not respond.

Why couldn't he tell my mom about the treatment plan? Why did he have to talk to Ricky in private? This made no sense. Mom was hurt and baffled.

Ricky was now starting to get very upset and agitated. Mom knew he needed to leave the room, so she told him, "Go sit in the car, Ricky. I will be right there."

He went to the car and my mom explained to Mr. Bonehead that she was afraid for him — and he was very dangerous. He said, "I cannot help you."

He proceeded to give my mom a business card with a crisis number on it.

"Mrs. Nau, if you just ignore Ricky and kick him out of your house, then he will get better," he said, his tone dripping with arrogance.

What? You can't ignore the mentally ill; they don't get better on their own! They need medication. What was wrong with these doctors and counselors telling a mother to abandon or ignore her child?

My mom was *furious!* As she was walking away from Mr. Bonehead, he yelled, "If he does anything, call the crisis number."

Mom yelled back angrily, "It will be too late. I will see you in the morgue!"

Her eyes filled with tears as she walked to the car and drove away.

After my mom and Ricky left the Santa Fe House, Mom bribed Ricky into going to McDonalds. One, she wanted to calm him down because he was upset and started showing signs of anger; and two, she was going to try to talk him into going back to the

Veterans Hospital.

After they ate, she was able to get him to agree to drive to the hospital. Once they got there, he would not get out of the car. Mom kept trying to encourage and persuade him to go in, "Come on Rick, it will be okay. They can help you get rid of the voices that you don't like. I will go in with you and help you."

Ricky refused and his anger peaked. "No! I don't want to go in! The medicine makes me sick! I want to go home, now!"

Ricky was extremely uptight and fidgety again. My mom was nervous and scared, so she drove home quickly.

On the way home, he started to hallucinate. He was yelling and pointing at traffic, "She's Satan! He's an alien! He's Jack the Reaper!"

Once again, he kept swiping his hand over the top of Mom's head to swipe away the demons and insects. Mom tried to break his thought pattern and settle him down by turning on the radio. However, it really did not help. He was very distracting, and she had a hard time driving home.

Once they got home, things continued to decline. Ricky was completely out of control with his hallucinations; he was yelling at the sky because he was hearing voices. His anger became more intense and lasted longer. His eyes became dark and blank. He kept swinging his fist into the air like he was hitting a punching bag.

He continuously paced and stomped in and out of the house and backyard, yelling respectively at the ceiling or sky. Everyone was home and very scared! We all felt anxious. We all felt like a bomb was about to drop. Ricky poked Jim a few times to see if he was real. Jim just ignored him. He also tried to start fights with Charlie, Bruce and me by pushing or yelling at us, but we all just kept our mouths shut and tried to stay away from him.

While Mom was loading the dishwasher, Ricky once again started poking her in the back to see if she was real. My dad heard my mom yell, "Ricky, stop it!" He rushed into the kitchen to protect her. Dad realized then that he had to keep his wife and the rest of his family safe. He told Ricky, "You either have to go to the hospital to take medication or leave and find another place to live."

Ricky did not respond. He just got very upset and continued to stomp around the house, ignoring my dad and family.

A little bit later, Mom and I heard Ricky call my sister to ask her if he could borrow $75 to travel. Based on his response, I assumed she said no because Ricky got very upset and slammed the phone down. I'm sure he hung up on her.

Ricky then proceeded to call the Littleton Police Department and tried to get my sister arrested. We heard him yell into the phone, "She is an alien from Mars! These aliens wrap people up in corncobs. You have to arrest her! She is insane! She is an abusive mom! That's what aliens do!"

I'm not sure what the police told Ricky, but he got angrier and slammed the phone down again.

Ricky's intensity grew. His fists were clamped tightly, and he had a dark, evil look on his face. When I looked at him I didn't even recognize him anymore because he had changed so much. He was not the person I knew and loved. It was frightening to watch. I can't explain what it is like to see a mentally ill person completely lose his mind. It's horrifying. All I wanted to do was leave the house.

My mom could see that Ricky was about to explode, so she called the police. He heard her on the phone so he went outside and stood across the street. He kept pacing back and forth on the sidewalk. The police arrived and my parents explained what was happening and how scared they were. The police went across the street to talk to Ricky.

"Ricky, is there a problem?" the officer asked.

"I'm not doing anything. I'm just standing here," he said calmly.

"Ricky, do you want us to take you to the hospital?" the officer continued.

"No, I'm not doing anything," he said, irritated.

"From my understanding, your family is worried about your health. Why don't you let us take you to the hospital?" the policeman offered.

Ricky now agitated, stated loudly, "You can't make me go!"

When the police came back over to my parents I could hear them say, "We're sorry," they said. "There was nothing we could do since he is not on your property, and he hasn't done anything violent."

"But he is sick," Mom said. "He will do something if we don't get help."

"Sorry, we can't arrest him," the officer said with concern. They knew this was a bad situation, but they were right, they could not arrest him unless he did something. So they left.

I was watching and listening to all of this out of my brothers' bedroom window. My heart sank when I saw them leave without Ricky. I was so tired of having tears in my eyes. I was tired of being scared. I was tired of Ricky! Why wouldn't anyone help us?

As soon as the police left, Ricky was so upset! He stormed furiously back into the house, running around from room to room, grabbing his stuff and sleeping bag. As he left the house, he shook his finger at Jim and berated him with hate, "I'm going to kill you! I'm going to burn down this house!" He slammed the door as he left.

We all stood there scared, knowing that these statements could be true. Needless to say, none of us slept that night. I could hear my dad walking around in the middle of the night checking each door and window to see if they were locked. I could also hear my brothers talking downstairs most of the night. We honestly did not know what to do. We just waited, worried and watched out for each other with no idea where Ricky went or when he would be back. I prayed in bed all night, "Please God, I beg you to protect my family and other people; please get Ricky some help; please help us, I beg you with all my heart. Please! Please! Please!"

CHAPTER EIGHT

The Day My World Collapsed

The next morning, Thursday, September 29th, Ricky came back home early. We do not know where he stayed the night before, maybe the park. Ricky kept knocking on the front door, asking my mom, "Let me in. I want to get something to eat and my clothes."

My mom would not let Ricky into the house. "Sorry, Rick, you can't come in. I'm not letting you in unless you go to the hospital," she said sadly.

"No, I can't go to the hospital; they will take my brain," Ricky said. "It's the spirits, Mom. They are making me crazy," he said trying to convince her.

"No, Ricky, I'm sorry. You can't come in," Mom yelled through the door.

Ricky was very delusional and hallucinating. He continued to make comments like, "I'm being hypnotized. My brain cells are being taken away." He also said, "Your food and water are poisoned."

Ricky also believed that Jim was not real and kept yelling at the door, "Mom, Jim is not real. You need to fingerprint him! He is an imposter!"

My mom was scared and sensed he was dangerous.

He left the doorway and started pacing back and forth in the front yard.

As Mom got ready for work, Bruce was about to leave for his first day at his new construction job. She told him, "Please go out the back door. I don't want Ricky in this house."

"Okay, I don't want to see him anyway," Bruce said.

As Bruce left out the back door to avoid Ricky, what he didn't realize was that Ricky had come around the backside of the house and surprised him at the door.

"Get out of my way!" Ricky yelled as he pushed his way into the house.

Bruce knew not to fight back. He could sense his brother was angry and distraught. Ricky came in to eat and gather clothes. Mom did not say anything to him. He just made a few comments in an angry, disturbed voice, "I'm going to leave. The spirits are making me crazy in this house. The aliens are invading your body."

My mom did not respond; she just kept an eye on him as she finished getting ready for work.

Ricky was nervous — he kept pacing the kitchen floor and his hands were shaking.

Mom had to leave to go to work at Eakers Clothing Store. She knocked on my door, "Debbie, I need to leave for work. I don't think you should stay here," she said.

Anxiously I replied, "I know, I'm leaving too!" I hurried and grabbed my backpack.

I left at the same time as Mom and got to school early. I would rather sit in the parking lot at school alone than to be left alone with Ricky. I was very scared and I wanted to avoid him as much as possible. Jim and Charlie were still downstairs sleeping when we left the house.

All morning, Ricky packed his clothes in a duffel bag and then he went out into the backyard. Jim watched him out of the kitchen window as he paced the backyard and yelled at the sky, "They're not real! They're trying to make me crazy! Stop telling me!"

Bruce happened to come back home — his new job was not ready for him to start. Jim decided to take Bruce to the store to get some more construction equipment for his new job while Charlie hung out downstairs to avoid Ricky.

By the time my mom came home for lunch around 11:15 a.m., Ricky's anger had escalated. As she entered the house nervously, not knowing what to expect, Ricky yelled, "Give me money! I want to leave. You are making me sick!"

Scared, Mom gave Ricky money. As she did so, she told him, "You cannot live in this house anymore, unless you go back to the doctors to get on medication."

"No! The doctors are crazy!" he yelled back at her.

Ricky started to back away from Mom as he pointed to her and cried, "There are scorpions crawling all around you!"

"Rick, it's part of your illness. Please let me take you to the hospital to get help," she pleaded with tears in her eyes.

"No! You're turning black!" he screamed as he continued to back away from her.

He was acting completely insane. Mom was afraid, frustrated and tired. She told Ricky as she was getting ready to go back to work, "You need to leave this house. Good luck, I hope you get help."

My mom knew in her heart that she should not go back to work, but she had no choice, there was no one to take her place that day. She was afraid to leave Ricky unattended. She also did not want to kick him out, but she knew she had no other choice. She had other children to protect. My mom left at 12:15 p.m. Jim and Bruce were still at the store, and Charlie was downstairs getting ready for work.

As these memories faded, my mind came back to the present moment. It was now 1:00 p.m. I stood in front of the glass door with Bruce watching Ricky sleep in the backyard.

All the memories of these last two years flooded my mind, which gave me an overwhelming feeling of sadness and an ache in my heart. My family had been through so much. I felt such a sick feeling in my body to be looking out at a young man who was once so vibrant, healthy and fun. Now he was a man plagued by mental illness and completely terrifying to be around.

Ricky looked pale, ghostly white, as though all the life had left his body; it was almost like his soul had left. Both Bruce and I turned and glanced at each other at the same time. His eyebrows were lifted and his eyes were large and filled with fear. We both knew something terrible was going to happen. There were no words exchanged between us; we just knew by our exchanged glance. Bruce understood clearly what I was thinking when I demanded that he lock the doors. He knew I was scared and didn't want Ricky in the house. I know he was scared too, because he had a sense of nervousness about him. His hand was shaking when he locked the door.

After the door was locked, I told him, "Don't let Ricky back into the house."

Bruce nodded, "yes."

I felt a little light-headed and shaky. I had a nervous twitch in my soul — a feeling I don't know how else to describe.

Jim got up out of the chair to see what we were doing. I told him, as we were looking out the window, "Ricky looks really bad! He looks dead."

"Yeah, he does," Jim said with deep concern.

"I don't think we should let Ricky back into the house," I said to Jim.

"Okay," Jim readily agreed as he stared at his brother.

"Let Charlie know," I said to Bruce because Charlie was downstairs.

I was so sick to my stomach; I thought I was going to throw up! I told Jim and Bruce, "I'm going to go lay down on my bed for awhile."

"I know what you mean. I don't feel good either," said Bruce.

Both Bruce and Jim went back into the living room. Bruce laid down on the couch while Jim sat in the chair. Out of the corner of my eye as I grabbed my backpack to go to my bedroom, I could see Jim's hand twitching and his foot tapping. I thought, *"we can't keep living our lives in fear of Ricky. It's going to kill us. Please help us God!"*

ᏗᏬᏏ

BANG! The sound of a bomb exploding in the air! I was startled and jumped out of my bed.

I ran to my bedroom door and tried to open it. I could not open it! It was stuck.

"Please God, open this door!" I screamed in my mind. What's going on? I was shaking the door, desperately trying to get out. I looked at my hands — and they were trembling. My chest tightened, and I felt like I was about to lose my breath.

I went back to my bed for a split second to sit down. I took a deep breath. I had to get out of this room now! I ran back to the door and tried again. Thank God it finally opened.

I ran out to the living room and screamed, "OH MY GOD! OH MY GOD!"

Jim was lying on his stomach on the floor next to a fallen chair in a pool of blood. I kneeled down next to him, grabbed his shoulders and leaned over his body to try to see his face. At that time, I went into shock, realizing Jim had been shot and there was a big hole in his back and there was blood everywhere!

He was trying to lean up. I screamed at him, "Stay down, I'll get help!"

He tried to turn his head to speak to me. I leaned down close to his face; I could hear the terror and pain in his voice as he whispered, "Get out of the house!"

Out of one corner of my eye, I could see Ricky and Bruce fighting on the front porch — and the gun lying by the front door. Out of my other peripheral, I could see blood running down the wall and blood all over the chair.

"Oh my God! Oh my God!" My thoughts gripped by frantic fear. *"What do I do? What do I do? I grab the gun and run... or call the police?"*

I decided that I had to help Jim. I got up, grabbed the phone and phone book, and ran to my bedroom.

Locking the door I jumped into my closet and slammed the door shut. I sat down on the floor of the closet, trying to hide underneath all my clothes, praying in the dark to God, *"Please God! Please God? Don't let Ricky find me! Please God!"*

Realizing it was too dark to see the phone book, I cracked the closet door open. I struggled to open the telephone book because my hand was shaking. I call the Littleton Police Department at 1:45 p.m. and quickly shut the closet door. I could hardly speak to the operator. My whole body was trembling and I could not get my voice out. I knew I could not speak loudly because I could not allow Ricky to hear me. I whispered to the operator, "My brother has been shot! Please help!"

"What is your location?" the operator quickly asked.

"Peakview Avenue," I said, shivering as my teeth started to chatter.

"Honey, what is your name?" the operator gently asked.

"Debbie Nau," I said, shaking and crying out of control.

"We are sending the police and ambulance right away!" the operator said.

I cried so hard that my shirt was soaked. I was trying so hard to be quiet and not to cry out loud. I could not let Ricky hear me!

The operator kept me on the phone, trying to calm me down. She kept reassuring me, "Everything will be okay. The police are on their way."

"Please help me!" I whispered.

"The police will be there shortly, it will be okay," the operator reassured me again.

There was a long silence.

I could not talk to her again. I just sat there in the dark, trembling and crying. It felt like an eternity. Every once in awhile she would ask, "Are you still there?"

I quietly whimpered, "Yes."

There was a long silence again.

In the background I could hear another operator state with urgency, "There has been another shooting on Peakview Avenue!"

A stinging pain shot through my heart as I cried uncontrollably. My knees were bent up to my chest and I put my face into my knees to muffle my deep cries. Thoughts were rushing in my mind, *"Oh my God! Oh my God! Who was shot? Where's Ricky? I can't let*

Ricky hear me! Oh my God! I can't breathe! My heart is hurting! Oh my God! Please help me!"

There was a long silence again.

BANG! BANG! BANG! I could hear the door shaking as Ricky was hitting and kicking it. He was trying to get into my bedroom. For a moment, time stood still. I thought I was going to die. A sharp pain clamped my head and bolted through the left side of my body. My eyes went blurry. I felt my arm go numb and heavy, and I could not move it. I dropped the phone on my lap no longer able to hold it. I had to pick up the phone with my other hand. Such intense pain seared through my head again — such horrendous pain. *"Oh my God! My head hurts! I'm going to die! Please God, please help me!"* I desperately prayed.

In a frantic whisper, I cried to the operator, "Ricky's kicking in the door! He's going to kill me! Please help me! I'm going to die." I held my breath. I didn't want Ricky to hear me. *"Please God, help me!"*

All of a sudden, it was quiet… a deadly silence.

I could not hear Ricky anymore.

I took a small breath of air. I sat there silently trying to listen to what was happening. The hairs on the back of my neck prickled as I realized Ricky was standing at my door listening intently to see if I was in there. I held my breath again, petrified. I closed my eyes, put my face into my knees and I was silent in the dark… the moment seemed to last forever.

Ricky moved away from the door. I could hear him walk into my parents' bedroom and move things around as though he was desperately looking for something. Next he went into the living room.

I heard a sad heartfelt cry and as he spoke to Jim, "I'm so sorry! I'm so sorry I shot you! I'm so sorry!" He kept apologizing and weeping. It was like I was hearing the old Ricky who I used to know.

Suddenly, he was quiet again and moments passed. His voice changed, it sounded deeper and demented as he unemotionally and coldly scolded Jim, "It's your fault! You're not real! You're an imposter!"

Chills ran down my spine when I heard him. I knew Ricky wasn't Ricky anymore.

Was he going to come back to my bedroom again? *"Oh my God, please don't let Ricky come back, Please don't come back!"* I prayed over and over.

In the distance, I could hear the wail of the ambulance sirens get closer. I knew help was on its way. I think that saved me from Ricky coming back to my bedroom. I then heard Ricky start running around the house, and grabbing things in a panic... and then it was silent again.

I started breathing again, and the operator told me, "The police and ambulance are almost at your house."

I started to shake vigorously and cry so loud that I felt like I was having convulsions. I released my silence. I screamed.

In a motherly soft voice the operator said, "It will be okay honey! They are almost there to help you. It's okay. You will be safe." As she gently tried to calm me down.

She eventually told me, "Honey, you have to leave your bedroom. The police have the house surrounded."

I didn't want to go out. I was terrified! I didn't know where Ricky was. I kept telling her, "No! I can't! I'm too scared!

"You have to leave the bedroom and come out of the house," the operator said.

"Can't the police come into the house and get me?" I cried hysterically.

She said, "No. You have to leave the closet and come out as far as you can with the phone and lay it on the floor. Then you need to walk out of the house. I will talk to you all the way out," she said with gentleness.

She continued, "The police will be there waiting for you."

I did not respond. I sat there quiet for a while to gather my courage to leave my room. I slowly opened the closet door and crawled out. I could hardly stand because my legs where shaking so badly. I went to the door and stood there for a moment. I was so terrified! What if Ricky was hiding in the house? What if he was downstairs and came back up? What if he was just standing right there? As my hand was trembling, I grabbed the doorknob, took a big breath, and slowly opened the door.

I slowly walked out of my room and peeked around the corner to see if Ricky was standing there. He wasn't. Thank God! I then slowly walked around the corner, and then I could see Jim again. *"Oh my God! Oh my God!"* I was crying uncontrollably again.

I pulled the phone up to Jim and rested it on the floor next to him. Ricky had turned Jim's body over. He was now lying on his back. There was a hole in his chest by his heart — and there was so much blood everywhere. I kneeled down next to Jim to see if he was still alive. I bent over and whispered to him, "I'm so sorry!" I got close to his face, and I put my arm around his stomach and my other hand on his shoulder as if was going to hug him. I looked into his eyes, and he looked at me then he looked at the ceiling. He continued to move his eyes around for a second.

I looked down at his chest. I saw it rise and then fall. It did not move again. I looked back into his eyes — and he now had a blank stare at the ceiling. He was lifeless. I saw him take his last breath. At that moment in time, I completely lost it and started to hysterically scream. I will never forget this moment for as long as I live!

Lost in time, I know I got up and walked out the front door, but I don't remember actually walking out. After I was out of the house and standing on the front porch, the Littleton SWAT Team (around ten members) was standing there, pointing their guns at me as though I was the killer.

They were screaming at me, "Get in the middle of the front yard!"

I was crying so hard I could hardly see, and I was trembling so badly, I could hardly walk.

The police kept yelling at me but I could not hear their words and I could not move my legs. Finally, a police officer ran up to me and grabbed my arm and dragged me to the middle of the street. Faintly in the background, I could hear the police officers yelling, "He still might be in the house! Go around to the side."

The police officer started to pull me toward the police car. I saw my neighbor Carol walking out of her house crying. She started to walk toward me, and I could tell she wanted to tell me something. I was crying so hard. I couldn't speak, and she could not speak either. We just stared at each other.

I knew in my heart at that moment someone else had died. I didn't know if it was Bruce or Charlie. I could tell by Carol's facial expression that it was bad. The police stopped Carol from talking to me and dragged me to the police car around the corner and put me in the backseat. I sat there for a while, all alone, and crying. I didn't know what was happening. I just heard so much commotion. I felt so empty. I felt so cold. I couldn't stop shaking.

Finally, a police officer came back to the car and asked me where my parents worked, and I told him. The police then drove me to the Littleton Police Station. I asked the driver, "What's happening?" He would not respond.

When we arrived at the police station, they led me into a white room where there was a wooden table with six chairs. They got me a glass of water, and one man said, "Just sit in here. We will be back later." I was left alone for a long time; it seemed like hours.

Every once in awhile someone would come into the room to see if I needed more water. I kept asking with anxiety as they entered the room, "Did someone else get shot? Who was it?" They would not answer me.

I just kept crying. I could not stop.

It was getting later in the day, and I had been at the station for hours. I overheard on the police radio that they had found Ricky and had arrested him. They were on their way back to the police station.

All of sudden a deep sense of fear overcame my body. I started to shake uncontrollably again. I was so scared to see Ricky. I just could not handle it.

At that time, two women police officers came into the room and told me, "We found Ricky, and we are bringing him in."

They could tell I was terrified. I just kept crying. They moved me into another room so I would not see him. The two women finally answered my questions. "We are so sorry. Your brother Bruce has been shot, and he died in the neighbor's house."

I was crying so hard, I could not breathe. My chest tightened and I gasped for air. One of the ladies rushed to my side and tried to coax me into breathing again. She kept trying to calm me down while she was rubbing my back. "Breathe. You need to breathe. Take one breath at a time. It will be okay."

With a weak, near silent whisper, I asked, "Where's Charlie?"

"We don't know. Who's Charlie?" they asked.

"Charlie is my brother. He was in the house when I went to lie down in my bedroom!" I said frantically.

One of the ladies became upset, jumped up, and ran out of the room to go make phone calls to find out where Charlie was. A deep sense of urgency filled the air.

I started to panic and prayed again, "Oh my God, please let Charlie be okay!"

I could hear them talking about Charlie on the police radio to see if they could find him. After awhile, one of the ladies came into the room and told me, "Charlie was not in the house or neighbor's house. We do not know where he is, but we feel that he is okay."

I was numb with shock. I started to hear commotion in the back room, and I knew Ricky was there. I just rested my head down on the table and continued to cry and ask, "Why God? Why?"

A few minutes later, they brought in our neighbor Carol for questioning. I know she saw Ricky there at the station, and it scared her to death. I wanted to run up and hug her, but officers would not let me speak to her. Through the glass window, I could see her face twisted in torment and fear. I could feel all the intensity that she was going through. I was sick to my stomach. I felt so bad that she had been caught up in the middle of our family's tragedy. *"I'm so sorry Carol!"* I thought.

It was close to 7:00 p.m. before my parents got to the police station to pick me up. They had been at the hospital with Charlie to identify the bodies. As I walked out into the lobby of the police station, I saw my parents come in. Trembling I ran to them crying so hard, I almost tripped myself. We were all crying and hugging each other.

My sister and her husband showed up minutes later at the police station. This is when I heard that Charlie was okay. My mom told me that he was with them at the hospital and was heading to my sister's house. I was so relieved to hear that. A deep sense of gratitude went through my body as I hugged my mom. I was so thankful to God for saving Charlie and me. It was surreal beyond description.

We left the police station and went to stay at my sister's house that night because we could not go home. I felt so sorry for my parents because they had to call and deliver the most horrible news to my brothers, Gene and Jeff. They also had to make other calls to family, friends and most importantly, to Carol. They had to find out what happened to Bruce.

As we turned on the TV that night, our family photo was on every major news station in Colorado, and the story of Ricky was being told. It was horrifying to see the footage of our house, pictures of Ricky being displayed and the news stations calling Ricky a murderer.

That night was the longest night of my life. None of us slept. We all just stared at the walls and ceiling, wondering why. I could feel Jim and Bruce's presences with us. I know they were there watching over us. This memory will always be embedded in my mind and soul. I knew I was changed forever.

CHAPTER NINE

Aftermath - A Single Event Can Change You Forever

As that night and the next two days unfolded, we were able to piece the story together from our neighbor Carol, the police and Ricky as to what had happened. Early that forenoon when my mom was at work, and Jim and Bruce were at the store, Ricky had searched my parents' bedroom and found my dad's deer rifles hidden underneath their bed. He pulled them out and hid them on the side of the house in a woodpile with all the bullets.

My dad had gotten rid of all the guns in the house months prior when we were starting to realize how dangerous Ricky was becoming. Dad hid his guns at his dear friend's house. Unfortunately, his friend's daughter was extremely depressed and had suicidal tendencies. The friend asked him to take the guns back in fear of his daughter finding them. My dad had only brought the guns back two days before Jim and Bruce died. He waited until everyone was asleep at night before he brought the guns back into the house, so no one would know. My dad thought the guns would be safe for a couple of days in his bedroom since none of us kids ever went into their room. He was going to try to find another friend to ask if he could store his guns at their house. Unfortunately, he never got the opportunity.

Sadly to say, when Ricky did search my parents' bedroom (probably looking for money), he found them. I feel such deep sadness for my dad and the guilt he must have felt. I know he would have moved the guns out of the house if he had another place to take them. We never imagined Ricky would actually load a gun and shoot it. I always imagined Ricky grabbing a knife and stabbing us because that would be a quick reaction to his anger. I just could not imagine him actually shooting someone. That would take forethought. It is so hard to comprehend that your brother would go to that extreme. No matter how bad he got, I still loved him deep in my heart, and I just didn't want to believe he would follow through even though my gut instincts told me otherwise.

Minutes before Ricky had shot Jim, Charlie came upstairs from the basement to leave for work. Looking out the back door, Charlie saw Ricky standing in the backyard, raging at the sky. Ricky saw Charlie at the door and seemed to be very mad and annoyed with him. Charlie sensed Ricky's irritations so he immediately left for work.

Ricky at that time must have walked to the side of the house, grabbed the rifle, and loaded it. He then walked around to the front of the house, went in through the front door, and shot Jim who was sitting in a chair in the front living room with Bruce.

Bruce was lying on the couch and jumped up to fight Ricky to get the gun away from him. They fought for a few seconds by the front door. Somehow Bruce was able to find the strength to get the gun away from Ricky. During this time I could not get out of my bedroom. I know my angels were protecting me because if I had walked out to the living room at that moment, Ricky would have shot me too.

Ricky then pulled a knife on Bruce — and the fight continued out the front door onto the porch of the house. The neighbors saw them fighting out of their windows. Bruce was able to get the knife away from Ricky. Bruce then ran to the neighbor's house for help. Ricky came back into the house right at the time I was leaving Jim to go call the police. Once again, he had ample opportunity to shoot me. Ricky grabbed the gun. He then chased and hunted Bruce down at the neighbor's house.

Bruce frantically banged on the neighbor's front door yelling, "HELP! HELP!"

Of course, Carol did not hesitate to let Bruce into her house. Petrified and in fear, Bruce told Carol and her brother, "Ricky shot Jim! Ricky shot Jim!"

"Oh, my God!" Carol screamed as she grabbed the phone to call the police.

Both Bruce and Carol's brother Jeff heard Ricky coming in through the front door of their house. They all looked at each other, fear gripping their souls. Bruce quickly ran downstairs, scrambling to find a place to hide. Jeff ran out the back door into the garage and backyard. Carol was left standing there with the phone in her hand.

As she turned around, Ricky was standing there, pointing the gun at her. Carol screamed "Oh, my God!" Ricky just stared at her. He intently looked her over as if he was seeing if she had horns on her head or a monster coming out of her.

Carol fell to the floor and hid underneath the kitchen table. Ricky at that time hit Carol hard in the forehead with the butt of the rifle. She continued to lie there underneath the table while she was holding the phone with the police on the other end.

Somehow Ricky knew that Bruce had gone downstairs. Ricky continued through the kitchen, staring and pointing the gun at

Carol, and he went downstairs to hunt and kill Bruce.

Carol could hear the doors slamming as Bruce was running from room to room. She could also hear Bruce begging Ricky. "Please don't shoot! Please don't do it, Rick! Please!" as he cried out with panic.

Ricky told Bruce with determination and no feeling, "Sorry, we could have been friends, but it's you or me!"

BOOM! A shot rang out.

As Ricky was coming back upstairs, Carol stood up from underneath the kitchen table and was still talking to the police on the phone. When Ricky reappeared in the kitchen, Carol remained frozen and did not say a word. Ricky just stared at her as he walked by. He didn't seem interested in hurting her. Carol told us he had a different look on his face than when he first entered the house. His determination to get Bruce was over.

At that time, Ricky came back to our house and tried to get into my bedroom. It was only by the grace of God that his temper had started to subside and the sounds of the sirens in the distance made him give up on his effort to kill me, too.

Bruce was alive and cognitive for a little while. Carol sat by his side and tried to help him. I'm so grateful to her. No words can express the sincere gratitude my family felt toward Carol for putting herself at risk and helping Bruce.

After the fire truck and ambulance got there, Carol kept yelling and telling them that Ricky had left the neighborhood. She continued to beg them to go into the house to help Bruce. The paramedics kept ignoring her, and they would not enter her house to give Bruce medical attention. They did not believe that Ricky had left the neighborhood. They kept thinking he was hiding, so they did not want to put any of themselves at risk of getting hurt.

It was very frustrating and shocking to Carol because Bruce

was bleeding to death and no one would help him. Ricky had shot him in the chest (lungs). The fire and ambulance personnel cannot go into to the house to help unless the police have given permission. Unfortunately, the police were delayed in getting to our house because a long coal train was going through Littleton and all the roads were blocked (due to this tragedy, that was all changed a couple years later and Littleton's main street bridge was built).

The SWAT team, which comes from another location, was at our house immediately. They too would not give permission to the paramedics to go into Carol's house to help Bruce. I didn't understand. They had guns! They could have escorted the paramedics into her house. Even at that time, other neighbors were telling them that Ricky had driven away. But no one would listen. The only thing the SWAT team did was point their guns at me and immediately clear the junior high school behind my parents' house in fear that Ricky might go over to the school to hurt the kids.

As I was being pulled away from my house, I wish the police would have allowed me to talk to Carol when I saw her on the street. Then I would have known it was Bruce who was shot, and I could have gone to be by his side. But the police held my arm tight as they dragged me to the police car.

After Carol had begged the paramedics to come into her house, and they ignored her, she knew she had to get back to Bruce to be with him and help him. They finally allowed her to return to Bruce, and she said the most beautiful thing happened. Bruce prayed to God, and he looked up over Carol's shoulder as if he was looking at someone. A deep sense of light, love and peace fell over Bruce's face as he said in a gentle, loving voice, "Oh, Jesus!" with a wonderful smile on his face. Carol could see the deep love in his eyes. He was seeing Jesus standing in front of him. At that moment, Bruce passed away.

My heart still hurts wishing I could have been there with him. It is such a blessing to me to know that Jesus was with him in his last moments. Tears still fall down my face just thinking about him and all he went through in those last terrifying minutes. He deserved to see Jesus.

When Ricky heard the police sirens in the distance, he had hurried and grabbed his stuff and took off in Jim's car. He drove over to another neighborhood not far from my parents' house. I think he just drove around because he did not know what to do or where to go. An hour or two later when the police found Ricky, he was quietly sitting in the car waiting. He didn't fight or try to escape. He just allowed the police to arrest him. He was not angry anymore and probably realized what he had done — basically, it was the calm after the storm.

While I was sitting in the car, the police came and asked me where my parents worked. I told them that my mom worked at Eakers Clothing Store just minutes from our house. The police went to the store and told my mom that there was a shooting, and they had to take her to the hospital. They would not tell her any more information than that.

The police then called my dad at his job and told him that he needed to get home. My dad had carpooled that day and his friend had to bring him home. When he got home, there were police and investigators running around and police tape all around the house. My dad knew that something terrible had happened, but he didn't know what. The police would not tell him anything, and they only stated that they needed to take him to the hospital.

Meanwhile, my mom told the police they needed to get in contact with Charlie's work and that they needed to get over to my sister's house because Ricky had threatened her the night before. They didn't know if Ricky was going to head over to her house or not. I believe the police called my sister and asked her to evacuate her house and go to the police station. My sister was babysitting other children at the time, so she had to contact all the other parents to come pick up their kids. Once the children had left, my sister and her husband went to the police station.

Not too long after Charlie arrived at work, his boss notified him that something had happened, and he had to go to the hospital. Charlie immediately left and drove over to the hospital to meet our parents.

As Mom and Charlie waited at the hospital, they didn't know what had happened, who it was, or if the person was still alive. My mom thought for a moment, that Ricky had killed himself. Finally, a reverend who worked at the hospital came and told them that two males believed to be Jim and Bruce has been shot — and they had died. The world stood still for moment, as their minds reeled with confusion. My Mom and Charlie went into complete shock and sobbed. The reverend asked my Mom and Charlie if they could go into the room to identify the bodies, but neither one of them could do it. They were paralyzed and bewildered, they could not move their legs. With shaking hands, my Mom gave some photos she had in her wallet of Jim and Bruce to the reverend, and he went into the room to identify the bodies.

When my dad arrived at the hospital, the policeman told him that the situation was bad. Dad rushed in to find Mom — and that's when he found out what had happened.

When they left the hospital, no words were said - only tears flowed. They were numb and could not believe what had happened. Somehow the police or someone drove my dad's car to the hospital (we still today don't remember how it got there) because my parents were able to drive away from the hospital, and Charlie drove to my sister's house.

I don't know how either my brother or my dad was able to drive. I don't think they even remember driving. I thank God that they did not get into a car accident. The police told my parents they could not go home because the house was taped off, and they were still doing the investigation. My parents had to drive to the store to get some toothbrushes and other items to take to my sister's house. My parents then went to the police station to pick me up and meet my sister and her husband. After we all hugged and cried, we all drove to my sister's house to stay for a few nights. Unfortunately, the confusing, sad and long mourning process of losing two brothers was about to begin.

Ricky's crime had made the headline news on all the news stations. Some of my friends heard on TV that afternoon what had happened and rushed over to my house to see if I was okay. They all stood around on the street trying to find out what had happened. They told me that there were news cameras everywhere. I also heard that Ricky was the first major mentally ill murderer in Littleton. It was definitely headline news, and it was splashed all over the papers the next day. Someone also told me that this story made national news. I don't know for sure if that was true, but I was surprised to hear it.

Friday morning we were all exhausted — none of us had slept. It was a long and tearful night. The phone rang constantly with family, friends and news stations. Even though Ricky was in the Littleton jail, I was still locked in traumatic fear. I could not be alone. I felt like I was always on the verge of an anxiety attack. I could not stop shaking, I was cold, and I had a hard time breathing, as though I could not catch my breath. My parents were busy getting Gene and Jeff airline tickets to fly home the next day.

They were also talking to the priest about the funeral. It was all a fog. No one knew what to do. We relied heavily on people helping us. It was such a desperately confusing time.

I was so numb, frightened and utterly exhausted. Mom made me lie down on the living room floor next to the couch, so I could be around everyone and not be alone. She covered me with a big blanket and put pillows all around me so I would feel secure. I tried fighting going to sleep — I was afraid of having nightmares, but I eventually passed out.

Later that afternoon, my close friends showed up at my sister's house to take me away from the hysteria. They were all so sweet and caring. We stayed the night at my friend Shelly's house, sat around and talked. I tried to explain what had happened, but how could I explain it all and the fear I felt? How could I explain that I went from the age of seventeen to forty in 3.3 seconds? How could I explain how bad it was to see your brother take his last breath and die in your arms? How could I explain how I survived and my brothers did not? So, I did not try. My friends would not have been able to understand anyway — they were only seventeen with no life experiences to compare. I realized at that moment that I was going to have to endure these feelings and sadly walk this road alone.

Otherwise, I can't really recall much more from that night; it's still all a blur. I think we went to another high school's football game just to get my mind off Ricky and the murders. I also think later that night some of my close guy friends came over to see me. I don't know for sure. I was glad to be away from the pain and confusion, I needed to be with friends and feel safe. I kept thinking over and over in my mind, *"If Ricky escapes jail, thank God he will not be able to find me."* Feeling safe and secure that night, I completely passed out while I was talking to my friends.

The next day was homecoming for my high school and the big football game. I was going to go back to my sister's house, but my friends talked me into going to the game. They said I needed some fun, and I still needed to keep my mind off Ricky. I felt very odd going to the game, afraid that people would wonder why I was there, and they would say bad things about me for showing up.

I eventually allowed my friends to talk me into going, and afterwards, I was glad. Everyone was very nice and supportive. Plus, it was my senior year and I didn't really want to miss the homecoming game. I saw my brother Charlie at the game. He was dating a friend of mine — and I was glad to see him. He needed to get away from the pain, too. I think he enjoyed the freedom of those moments as much as I did. The next couple of days were going to be very difficult. We were going to go see Ricky in jail the next day and view Jim and Bruce at the mortuary. Monday was the funeral. A few hours of escape at a football game made it somewhat tolerable.

I did not sleep that night. I kept replaying every moment of Thursday's events over and over again in my head. I could not get the vision of Jim's bloody body lying on the floor, taking his last breath, out of my head. Nor could I rid myself of the terror of the image of Ricky trying to get into my bedroom.

I also had deep fears of seeing Ricky in jail the next day. What would it be like and what would I say to him? I was terrified of going to sleep. I laid in bed with the lights on because I was so scared of the dark and what I would see. Mentally and physically exhausted, all I kept thinking was, *"God, please help me through this!"*

On Sunday, October 2nd, I watched the sunrise through the window. This forenoon as a family, we were all going to go visit Ricky in jail to show our love and support. It was a very scary moment for me — to go into a jail cell and look into Ricky's eyes. I didn't know what to expect. Did he know what he had done? Would he apologize? Would he be angry and try to attack us? I just didn't know what to think, and deep in my heart, I really didn't want to go.

When we arrived at the police station, all the officers were very sincere and helpful and ushered us around. Their sincere sorrow was obvious. We went into a locked and secured hallway. Down the hall, I could see Ricky sitting in his cell. I could tell he was very happy to see us. It was like he was afraid we had abandoned him, and he had just discovered we did not. It was a surreal feeling wanting to hug him and tell him I loved him, at the same time, overwhelmed by fear and anger, wanting to scream at him for what he had done.

The whole family entered the cell cramped close together. Amazed, I watched my Mom immediately embrace Ricky with an intense hug. Both of my parents told Ricky that they loved him and they would be there for him. The rest of us stayed silent and astonished as we witnessed two parents showing deep love and compassion for their son.

Suddenly, I felt a deep sense of fear and evil in the room. I can't explain it, but it felt like something was around Ricky. I know other family members felt it, too. It was very uncomfortable. I can't recall all of what Ricky said, but I do know he apologized and tried to suggest that Jim was not real, and that he was trying to save him. I remember my mom crying while I stood quietly in the corner. I was actually hiding behind my brother and brother-in-law. I was frightened of Ricky, and I didn't want to be close to him. My feelings were in deep turmoil as in one moment I was angry and scared, and then the next moment, I felt sympathy and love for him. As my anxiety grew I started to fight back the bile that was rising in my throat. I fought throwing up and fainting as I grabbed my brother's arm with one hand and held my other hand against the wall for support. All I kept thinking was *"please God, get me out of here before I lose it!"* We didn't stay long, thank goodness, but Mom and Dad wanted to show Ricky that he still had a family.

Two court-appointed psychiatrists interviewed Ricky that weekend to determine if he was mentally ill or sane for his court date that followed a few days later. From reading the psychiatrists' reports, I learned what Ricky had been experiencing that day and why he killed Jim and Bruce.

Ricky truly believed in his heart that Jim was an imposter or a replacement. He thought that evil spirits or aliens had taken over his body. He believed that the real Jim was hiding in another place in Colorado. Ricky thought he could save Jim by killing his replacement. He also thought Jim was corrupted by another god in Vietnam, and this other god was going to take over America. Ricky thought his life was in danger. He thought his brothers were going to take eternity away from him and control him. He was convinced that they were going to crucify him. Ricky heard a voice that sounded like Jim's voice, and it said it was going to kill him and populate the world with purple bats and demons. Ricky thought that both Bruce and Jim were taking his soul. He believed that killing them would give them salvation of their souls.

Ricky also believed he was Jesus, and that they shared the same brain structure. Ricky had a war going on in his head about good and evil. He also thought he had leprosy, the telephones were tapped, people were watching him, and poison gas was in his food. This is the quote that was taken from Ricky while they were interviewing him for court:

"I asked the lawyers — I wanted to have a fingerprint check on my brothers. I think the Revolutionist Government took my brother and had him replaced. I am being psyched-out by everybody. It is just another word for darkness growing. The world is so full of darkness. I became one of God's knights fighting against darkness. He might be my brother in appearance, but he is really Jack the Ripper. My mother thinks she is someone else. Every time I look at her I see someone else. We are all being controlled by spirits. The spirits made me shoot my brothers because I had to save the universe. I really don't think it was my same brothers. It would have been somebody who had facial changes and everything else. I saw my brother one day, he had a short stubby nose. The next day I saw his nose was perfect again. I am God's knight. If I get off this planet and have any soul left, I will make it to another planet. I can also pick up other individuals' thoughts, being able to intercept messages that were being transferred from one person to another. Maybe I am Jesus."

Ricky truly believed all these thoughts. It is hard for us to understand and comprehend. He really did think he was saving Jim and Bruce. He just didn't understand what was real, or how badly he had this terrible brain disease. Three days later, the court system quickly committed Ricky to a lifetime sentence in the Colorado State Mental Institution in Pueblo.

Furthermore, in court, the judge asked Ricky why he didn't kill Carol. He told the judge, "She thought I was God." This notion came from the statement she made when he walked into her house, and she said, "Oh my God!" Ricky thought he was God, and since she knew that, he did not kill her. That statement saved her life.

Later that day, we had to go to the mortuary to view Jim and Bruce. With my stomach still in knots, I throw up in the bathroom prior to leaving my sister's house. Trembling with fear over seeing them for the first time when I got to the mortuary, I stood out in front for a little while. I could not get my nerve up to walk in through the front doors. My mom had to come outside to coax me in.

"It's okay. There is nothing to be afraid of. We are all going in together. I know this is very hard, but if you don't see them you might regret it later," she said.

"I'm too scared. I don't want to go in," I blubbered with tears in my eyes.

"I'm here with you and so is your dad. Why are you afraid?" Mom asked gently.

"I don't know. Dead bodies scare me," I said full of apprehension.

"They're not going to hurt you. They will look peaceful and they're in heaven now. Come in with me; we will go in slowly," she said as she gently held my hand and arm as we walked in, side by side.

When we walked inside, there was a waiting area. Everyone was standing there waiting for us before they entered the room. It felt horrible to me! I was dreading every moment.

My brother Charlie and I walked in together. Charlie almost collapsed when he saw his brothers. I grabbed his back and arm and held him tight. He cried so hard he could barely walk. My tears were so intense I could not see where we were walking. I just held on to Charlie and slowly followed the colored shirt in front of us.

Seeing Jim and Bruce was like a hard slap on the face with reality. For the last two days we had been living in shock and confusion. Almost like watching a very slow motion movie of yourself where you could not feel, touch or move. All you could do is watch and ask; is this really happening? Is this all a bad dream? Now, seeing them, we knew - yes it was real! It was a very painful recognition. The whole family was having a very difficult time. At first, we were confused about who was who. The mortuary messed up and put the wrong suits on each of them. I was expecting to see Bruce in his pretty blue-grey suit and Jim in his brown suit. But when I walked up to Bruce's coffin, it confused me because it was Jim in the blue suit, and Bruce was in the brown suit. It was hard because I had mentally tried to prepare for what I was going to see, and then it was something different. I will never forget that moment. I still can remember it as if it was yesterday.

That night I slept at my friend's house. All of our family and friends had come into town for the funeral. My friend Stacy was very supportive and helped me through that night. She knew I was scared of the dark and the nightmares, so she left her light on, rubbed my back, and stroked my hair, a nurturing mother taking care of a child until I fell asleep. So gripped by anxiety, I was having a hard time relaxing. I was very grateful for her kindness and help to get me through this difficult situation.

The next morning she helped me get ready for the funeral. We drove to my parents' house, which was hard because it was the first time back at the house since that day. We sat in the car for a few moments before I was able to walk up to the front door. I had to get some clothes to wear for the funeral. We also went there to meet and pick up Charlie.

I didn't know what to expect when I walked in. I didn't know how I was going to feel or what I was going to see. My hand was shaking when I grabbed the doorknob and I paused for a second to take a breath before I opened the door. I visually saw Jim lying there on the floor when I walked in. I saw a large section of the carpet torn away and a hole in the wall. The chair was gone and there was a big empty spot. It absolutely broke my heart. I tried extremely hard to be strong, so Stacy and Charlie would not see what I was seeing or feeling. I hurried to my bedroom as fast as I could to change my clothes as I quietly wept. I had a hard time putting on my clothes because my hands were shaking so badly. My family had already left for the mortuary to get ready for the funeral procession. I hurried as fast as I could just so I could get out of that miserable house.

When we arrived at the mortuary, I went back inside to say goodbye to Jim and Bruce. We all put different items in their coffins for memories. I was doing okay at first but when I saw them close the coffins, I lost it, and I started to cry uncontrollably again. Knowing it was the last time I would ever see them, it freaked me out. I did not want to say goodbye. I wanted them to be alive! *"Please God, let this be a bad dream,"* I kept thinking. I cried all the way to the church.

I don't remember much about the funeral. I went into a comatose-like state; walked where I was supposed to walk, and sat where I was supposed to sit. I just followed my family wherever they went. I didn't hear a word of the funeral and had no idea what music was played. I just sat there and stared at the two coffins. It was a big funeral with lots of people. I do remember seeing the

My family the day after the funeral.
We were all extremely exhausted and put on fake smiles to say good-bye to my cousins.
L to R: Charlie, Mom, Theresa, Jeff, Gene, Debbie, Dad

news cameras across the parking lot when we left the church to go to the gravesites, but that is all I remember. Friends told me that the funeral procession was several miles long. We had lots of support and people who cared. Looking back now, I wish I would have paid closer attention and soaked up all those detailed memories; but I guess I did the best I could under the circumstances.

I did not return to school for a week. The days and months to follow were the hardest time of my life. The grieving process was very difficult and everyone in my family handled it differently. I was fighting depression, nightmares, and physically feeling sick most of the time. I missed Jim and Bruce, so much, especially Bruce. We were only two years apart and had been much closer than Jim and I.

For the next three months, I lived at my friend Shelly's house. I was having too much difficulty living at home with the memory of Jim's death. I was so grateful to her and her family for opening their home and hearts to me. They were always kind and loving and made me feel safe and secure since I had a hard time going home to visit my parents. Seeing the reminders of Jim and Bruce all over the house was just too much for me at that time. It took me a long time to work through those feelings.

School was also tough. I could not concentrate. I didn't fit in, and no one understood what I was going through. My senior year was an awful year! I wanted to feel normal, like a teenager, but I felt so old and tired. I felt pulled in many directions. I wanted to be that teenager who fits in and is invited to parties; I wanted to be that fun and likeable friend; I wanted to be a supportive sister; and I wanted to be an understanding daughter. But in reality, I was withdrawn, confused, lonely, scared, sad and most importantly, I felt survivor's guilt. I just didn't know how to deal with all of those emotions. So I kept to myself most of the time and missed out on all the fun activities and parties.

I don't know how I kept my grades up, but I did. I guess I wanted so badly to graduate so I could move on, go to college, and get out of my parents' house. I also loved and missed Ricky. It was a strange roller-coaster ride of feelings when it came to him. I never stopped loving him, but I did feel angry toward him for taking away our brothers and my childhood. High school was supposed to be the best time of my life. I always wondered, would I ever feel better? Would it ever get easier? Would I ever forget? These questions haunted me every day.

A year later, my questions were answered. I was in college, and I came home for the weekend because it was Jim and Bruce's first year anniversary. It was a warm and beautiful fall day. The sun was shining and the leaves were turning yellow and orange. I could smell fall in the air but I was feeling depressed, lost and confused, and I wasn't sure if my beliefs were still there. I was losing faith in God.

I remember going outside in my parents' backyard and sitting on their deck. Tearful and angry with deep desperation and sadness, I looked up into the sky and cried out loud to God, "Will I get better? Will I heal? Will my family be okay? Will the nightmares stop? Will I forget the vision of Jim?" I pleaded with God to please talk to me and give me some type of sign. I asked Him to send me a dove, so I would know He really did exist and that He heard my prayers.

A few minutes later, as I was sitting there crying and feeling deeply sad and empty, two beautiful white doves flew down and landed right in front of me. They just looked at me and cooed for a few minutes. They didn't seem to be scared of me. I was wide eyed! Is this really happening? God didn't send me just one dove; he sent me two to represent Jim and Bruce. I really couldn't believe what

I was seeing. I really was not expecting God to hear me or send me the sign I had requested. I knew at that moment that things were going to be okay. God was with me, I was going to heal, and my faith was restored. That was the first day I started the healing process of mourning Jim, Bruce and Ricky. I thank God every day for that moment because it was truly a beautiful blessing that I desperately needed.

Two Littleton Brothers Slain; 3rd Is Arrested

By GEORGE LANE
Denver Post Staff Writer

Tragedy struck a large, close-knit Littleton family Thursday when one of the sons allegedly shot two of his brothers to death.

Police said the 22-year-old man fatally wounded one brother at their home, then chased the second brother to a neighbor's house and shot him to death also.

The two men died at Swedish Medical Center. The brother accused of the shooting was arrested about three hours later by Cherry Hills Village police.

The victims were identified as Jim Nau, 20, and Bruce Nau, 32, both of 746 W. Peakview Ave. Police identified the suspect as Richard Jay Nau, 22, of the same address. Richard Nau was being held Thursday night in Arapahoe County Jail for investigation of first-degree murder.

Littleton police first received a call shortly before 2 p.m. Thursday from a woman who said someone had been shot at 746 W. Peakview Ave. The caller later was identified as Deborah Nau, a teenage sister who wasn't injured.

About the same time police received a call from another woman who reported that a man had just run into her home at 796 W. Peakview Ave. and shot a man.

Officer Dan Stocking of the Littleton Police Department said officers rushed to the neighborhood and found wounded men at both addresses.

"We thought the suspect was still in the house," Stocking said. "The houses are right in back of Euclid (Junior High) School, so we evacuated all of the students in the classrooms closest to the houses."

After a search turned up no one, the students were allowed to return to classes and a description of the suspect was broadcast to all area police departments.

Richard Nau was arrested by Cherry Hills police just before 5 p.m. in the 3800 block of South Albion Street.

Please See KILLINGS on 19-A

KILLINGS From 1-A

Thomas Mason, who lives at 796 W. Peakview Ave. where the second shooting took place, said his daughter made the second call to police. He wasn't home at the time.

"Only thing I can think of is the boy came down here looking for help," Mason said. "He knew someone would be home, there always is."

Mason said his children knew the Nau brothers "because the families have been here a long time. We all knew each other."

He said he wasn't aware of any problems at the house and knew of no bad blood between the family members.

However, a neighbor who asked not to be identified "because I know the family too well," said there had been problems "back and forth" with Richard.

The young woman said the Naus had a large family — six boys and two girls — and she had gone to school with several of them.

Mrs. Jean Jacobson, who lives at 776 W. Peakview Ave. — the house between the two murder scenes — said that Richard had been in the service, and she said he had changed when he returned home.

"Of course the boy was ill. He has been awfully antagonistic," Mrs. Jacobson said. "Before that, all was fine.

Two brothers dead; third held in shooting

W. Peakview Avenue man held in shooting deaths at separate homes. No motive established

By Stephen Olver

Two Littleton brothers are dead and a third behind bars following a double shooting Thursday afternoon at two homes on W. Peakview Avenue.

The bodies of James Nau, 32, and Bruce Nau, 20, were found in nearby Peakview Avenue homes with fatal gunshot wounds to the chest at about 2 p.m. Thursday. Charged in their killings is 22-year-old brother Richard who was apprehended by police 2½ hours later while driving in Cherry Hills Village.

Littleton Police still have no motive for the killings which rocked the usually quiet sidestreet and forced the partial evacuation of adjacent Euclid Junior High School while the suspect was still at large.

Police spokesman Steve Johnson said the first report of the shootings came in at 1:57 p.m. from 746 W. Peakview — Richard's home. As police responded to the report, a second call came from 796 W. Peakview where a woman said two men had burst into her home with one shooting the other with a rifle. The gunman then fled in a 1971 brown Chrysler, she told police.

Police officers arrived to find both shooting victims dead in the separate homes. An all-points-bulletin reached Cherry Hills Village police officers who spotted a car matching the description of the 3800 block of S. Albion Street at 4:45 p.m. Richard Nau surrendered without incident and was taken to the Littleton Police Station where he stayed for several hours before being transferred to the Arapahoe County Jail.

Nau was ordered held without bond Friday morning and will appear Oct. 5 in District Court to enter a plea.

"We have no idea of the motive," Johnson told The Independent Thursday night after the shooting of the brothers who all three lived the 746 W. Peakview address. The first call to police from the home apparently was made after the 20-year-old brother Bruce was shot. *(See photo p.*

LITTLETON RESIDENT RICHARD J. NAU is transported from police headquarters to the Arapahoe County Jail Thursday night after being taken into custody in the shooting death of his two brothers. The bodies of James and Bruce Nau were found in separate homes on W. Peakview Avenue Thursday afternoon. Richard was apprehended almost three hours later while driving in Cherry Hills Village.

David Ake/The Independent

Nau in Mental Hospital 2 Days Before Slayings

By FRED GILLIES
Denver Post Staff Writer

A Littleton man described by his family as suffering from schizophrenia that conjured hallucinations of demons, scorpions and the devil was released from a mental hospital two days before he allegedly shot two of his brothers to death, The Denver Post learned Friday.

Richard Jay Nau, 22, was removed from his home by Littleton police a week before the shootings, was taken to Arapahoe Mental Health Center for an evaluation, and then was placed in Colorado State Hospital in Pueblo,

only to be released three days later, according to police documents and other sources.

Meanwhile, Nau's parents said their son had been without medication necessary to control his mental illness since a judge last July ruled that the medication wasn't needed.

"We tried frantically in the last few days to get him in the hospital," said Gerald Nau, father of the suspect. "He had schizophrenia and he was a very sick boy."

The judge's ruling "was the thing that was so crushing," the suspect's mother, Elnore Nau,

Please See NAU on 11-A

Nau Had Been in Mental Hospital

NAU From 1-A

said in an interview Friday night. "How can a judge who knows nothing about this make a ruling when a psychiatrist says Rick needs medication so bad?"

Neither parent could identify the court or the judge who made the decision.

From July until Thursday, when Nau's two brothers were killed, Richard Nau was without medication, his parents said. In the most severe moments of his illness, they said, he was seeing demons coming out of the wall, scorpions around his mother, and he believed certain persons — including one of his brothers — were possessed with the devil.

Nau was being held Friday in Arapahoe County Jail for investigation of first-degree murder in connection with the shooting deaths of his brothers, Jim, 32, and Bruce, 26, on Thursday afternoon. One brother was shot at the family's home at 746 W. Peakview Ave. and the other was fatally wounded at a neighboring home.

The suspect was advised of his rights Friday morning and then ordered held without bond by Arapahoe County Court Judge Richard Cesaboom. Formal charges are to be filed at 8:30 a.m. Wednesday in Littleton District Court.

According to Mrs. Nau, this is what happened on Thursday — the day of the shootings:

"He knocked at the door . . . and came in. He was hallucinating — a schizophrenic is paranoid and can't control their temper or thoughts. I went to Mass and returned. He was whisking around, a little hyper, not thinking too well. I went to my sales work, and then came home for lunch. He was packing his backpack. He was kinda staring, he was seeing demons coming out of the walls. I knew he was not in

Nau leaving Arapahoe County Court.

from his home at the Peakview Avenue address because he "was causing problems." The report notes further that Nau's parents requested that he be evaluated and placed in a hospital.

Thomas Machiarletti, executive director of the Arapahoe Mental Health Center, confirmed Friday that as a result of the center's evaluation of Nau on Sept. 24, "we recommended hospitalization" of Nau at the Colorado State Hospital in Pueblo. Machiarletti said he had been advised by the center's attorney not to make any further comment.

Littleton police and the Arapahoe district attorney's office couldn't provide details Friday on the length of time Nau remained in the state hospital or when he was released. Guy Mayo, assistant superintendent for administrative services at the State Hospital, said Friday he was unable to provide any information on

get him in other hospitals, and they were full. Then they took him to the hospital in Pueblo.

"He was only there until Tuesday. A psychiatrist said, 'I don't know why the boy is here. There is nothing wrong with him.' They brought him to a halfway house (run by Arapahoe Mental Health Center) on South Santa Fe Avenue. It's a volunteer program and you don't have to do anything.

"Rick came home Wednesday . . . I said, 'Rick, it can't go on like this . . . , you have to take your medication and go to the halfway house and stay there, or go to the Veterans Hospital as an outpatient.'

"On Wednesday, he went to the Veterans Hospital, but wouldn't go in and get his medication and he came back home. I said he would have to go to the halfway house until he got the medication and he could bring it home and take it under my supervision.

"But he wouldn't leave home, and I called (Littleton) police. I asked police if they would hold him for a while while I called the Veterans Hospital to get him back in. But police said they couldn't do anything because he hadn't done anything. Then he walked away, and I don't know where he went."

Their son, the parents said, was in the Navy for 1½ years and during that time was in Japan for one year. He received an honorable discharge in 1981, but the Navy said he suffered from extreme anxiety and wasn't suited for military service and couldn't come back into the Navy, his parents said.

After returning home from Navy service, he was "hallucinating pretty bad," his mother said. An application for a disability was filed and granted by the Veterans Administration, and he received a $350 per month disability pay

Frantic effort to get help fails to avert tragedy

Littleton man held in death of brothers

By Shirley Smith
Sentinel Writer

Gerald Nau spent nearly a week seeking psychiatric help for his 22-year-old son Richard, but that week of frantic need ended in tragedy when Richard Nau was arrested in connection with the shooting of his brothers James, 32, and Bruce, 20, on the afternoon of Sept. 29.

Nau is being held in the Arapahoe County Jail without bond. He is to be charged Wednesday (today) with two counts of first degree murder, according to Littleton Police Detective Dan Rupp.

Rupp said neighbors near the Nau home at 748 W. Peakview Ave. heard shooting that Thursday afternoon. Nau apparently was arguing with his brothers, according to police.

Bruce Nau ran to a neighbor's house and told Carol Mason that Richard had shot

LITTLETON — Frantic attempts by a man to get psychiatric help for his son failed to avert tragedy last week in a quiet West Peakview Avenue neighborhood. Richard Nau, 22, is being held in the Arapahoe County Jail on suspicion of shooting to death his two brothers, James, 32, and Bruce, 20. In a related story, Arapahoe officials explain how involuntary confinement of mental health patients is restricted by state laws.

NAU

PAGE 2

Law restricts mental health care options

Sept. 24, when the Gerald Nau family were at their wit's end with the mental condition of their son Richard, now in jail in the investigation of the murder of two of his brothers on Sept. 29, they called the Littleton Police Department.

Police arranged for an evaluation by the Arapahoe Mental Health Center. Richard voluntarily agreed to go to the Colorado State Hospital in Pueblo, but Nau left after a brief stay.

Nau was back in the family home when the tragic shooting occurred, according to Littleton police.

Families in Arapahoe and Douglas Counties with a member experiencing any number of mental problems can turn to the Arapahoe Mental Health Center.

There is just so much the center can do.

Laws mandate what it can accomplish, according to Executive Director Ron Machlorietti.

The director refused to talk about the Nau case specifically, but he did discuss Arapahoe Mental Health Center's process in general.

"Some people say, 'Can't you just lock Susie up?' If she acts strange or different. It's not against the law to act different. The Colorado Revised Statute is fairly specific on criteria for assessment. If a person is gravely disabled, unable to care for themselves, 'imminently' dangerous it may be possible to put them on a mental health hold.

"The real issue is what is the least restrictive setting a person can be in. Fifteen years ago the population in state mental hospitals were much larger. But individuals have inherent rights protected by laws," Machlorietti said.

Machlorietti said the center can be called in to do evaluations by the police, social agencies, referrals and they are

done by staff members, including psychiatrists, psychologists, licensed social workers and psychiatric nurses.

The process consists of gathering as much information about the person as possible and a face-to-face evaluation. The staff makes a recommendation, which might be hospitalization, out-patient treatment, or a stay in a facility such as Littleton's Santa Fe House.

"Services can be offered on a voluntary basis, but if a person doesn't want help it's a frustrating situation."

The director said sometimes the center cannot respond to services an individual is asking for. "We can't provide it."

Families can get caught in situations where the mental health aid offered doesn't measure up to the situation as they see it.

"We share their frustration," he said.

Frantic effort to get help
fails to avert tragedy

Continued from page 3

James. She called Littleton police at 1:57 p.m., Rupp said. Richard allegedly followed Bruce, who fled to the basement of the Mason home. Mason heard a shot, then Richard left the Mason home and drove off in James' car, according to Rupp. Richard was arrested by Cherry Hills police later that afternoon.

James and Bruce were pronounced dead at Swedish Medical Center. They had both been shot once in the chest with a deer hunting rifle.

Rupp said Debbie Nau, a senior at Arapahoe High School, also called police. The young woman was taking a nap when she heard a shot and discovered her brother James lying in the living room. She locked herself in her room and called police.

RICHARD NAU is a graduate of Heritage High School and was a goalie on the hockey team. "He was a good team player," recalled a man associated with the team at the time.

Gerald Nau said after high school Richard enlisted in the Navy and while he was in Japan "his letters began to get real strange. No sooner did that happen than Richard was sent home." It was explained that he was in a state of "extreme anxiety" and his discharge was "for the good of the service."

Nau described his son as "schizophrenic."

"When he came home he spent some time in the veteran's hospital. He got somewhat better."

Town meetings set

The Arapahoe County Republicans will have a town meeting in the Littleton area to allow elected officials to communicate with citizens by answering questions and listening to concerns.

Rep. Dan Schaeffer is expected to attend the meeting from 7 to 9 p.m. Oct. 12 at Bemis Library, 6014 S. Datura St.

Nau said his son would not take his medication. His condition devastated the family, Nau said. At one point they went to court, but, Nau said, "the judge in his infinite wisdom said Richard could not be forced to take his medicine. It violated his rights."

On Saturday, Sept. 24, "things got really bad," Nau said. The family tried to get him in Veteran's Hospital, but there wasn't room. They called the Littleton police who called Arapahoe Mental Health Center for an evaluation. Richard went voluntarily to the Colorado State Hospital in Pueblo. His stay was short-lived as was a brief time at Santa Fe House in Littleton.

Wednesday, Sept. 28, Richard was back at the family home, Nau said. The family called police again and asked if they could put Richard in detention. "They said, 'We can't do it,' " Nau commented.

Rupp said, "We can't just arbitrarily put people in jail."

"I TOLD RICHARD, 'You can't stay here if you don't take your medicine. Go down to the vet's (Veteran's Hopsital) and get your medicine and take it under my supervision.' He went down to the vet's, but he wouldn't go in and get it," Nau said.

Wednesday night Richard did not come home. The shooting occurred Thursday afternoon while the elder Nau was at work.

Elnore and Gerald Nau have lived in Littleton 19 years and were parents of eight children. Gerald Nau worked for Western Electric and Elnore Nau had a part-time job at a local department store.

James Nau, born Aug. 8, 1951 in Omaha, was the eldest child. He graduated from Littleton High School. He was a Vietnam veteran and had been working in Alaska on a fishing boat and was to go to Vancouver to a herbology school, his father said.

Bruce Nau was born June 8, 1963 in Omaha and attended Heritage High School. He had just landed a construction job, according to Nau.

Nau charged today in brothers' deaths

By Linda Dowlen Roberts

Richard Nau, suspect in the Sept. 29 shooting deaths of his two brothers, was charged today with two counts of first degree murder. He will be facing a sanity hearing and pleading later today.

Nau, 746 W. Peakview Ave., was arrested Sept. 29 after police found the bodies of his brothers, James, 32, and Bruce, 20, in two nearby homes. Both brothers had been shot in the chest.

Nau was allowed to refuse medication for his diagnosed mental illness three months earlier. He had been determined to be mentally ill but not irrational or illogical in not allowing himself to be treated with Loxitane, an antipsychotic drug, according to a July 26 court ruling by Littleton District Court Judge Robert F. Kelley.

"The evidence has not established any emergency that would justify the necessity of repeatedly forcibly injecting (Nau) with Loxitane," Kelley said.

Nau is being held without bond in the Arapahoe County Jail, awaiting an Oct. 5 district court hearing.

Three months before the deaths of his brothers, Nau won a petition to have the right to refuse medication while he was being treated for mental problems at the Veterans Administration Hospital. At the time of the hearing, Nau told the court that he was at the hospital on a "voluntary" basis but admitted he was being held under a court order on a locked ward.

According to court records, Nau had been diagnosed last July as a paranoid schizophrenic who was dangerous to himself and to others. After being discharged from two years of military service because of his mental condition, Nau had been hospitalized six times. Records state he had been out of the hospital for five months before he was taken to the VA hospital June 24 following a family disturbance at his home. Nau had allegedly been fighting with his father.

On July 12, he reportedly escaped from the VA Hospital but was apprehended at his parents' home by police, according to court records. He was returned to the hospital.

During the hearing Nau, who considers himself to have a severe nervous condition, objected to the hospital's use of Loxitane in his treatment, saying it gave him side effects such as "eyes popping out of his head," "brain felt like a rock," and "it was a strain to remember." Nau also said the drug made him depressed and gave him trouble with his eyesight. He said he felt taking the drug was akin to alcohol abuse.

Slay suspect sought help

Hospital released brother of victims

By ARNOLD LEVINSON
Rocky Mountain News Staff Writer

Richard Jay Nau sought help at the state hospital. He is a suspect in the deaths of his brothers.

LITTLETON — Five days before he was accused of killing two of his brothers, Richard Jay Nau threatened them and then checked into the Colorado State Hospital in Pueblo.

Littleton police said Friday they thought he was still there when his brothers were shot to death.

"It appears that Pueblo (State Hospital) let him go, and it appears that Pueblo made a terrible mistake," said a source close to the case, asking not to be named.

Nau, 22, is being held without bond for investigation of first-degree murder in the killing Thursday of his brothers James, 32, and Bruce, 20. Officials will decide next week whether he will be charged.

Nau was screened Sept. 24 by Arapahoe Mental Health Center staff after his parents sought police help, saying he had threatened to kill his brothers.

He voluntarily went by ambulance from the Littleton police station to the State Hospital, Detective Dan Rupp said.

"We all thought he was still down there when this happened," Rupp said Friday. "I think somebody's in trouble, to say the least."

Although hospital officials refused to discuss the case, it was learned that Nau was released Tuesday night or Wednesday. His brothers were killed Thursday. James in the family home and Bruce in the basement of a neighbor's house, where he had fled.

Tom Macolletti, director of the Arapahoe Mental Health Center, confirmed that Nau's screening and hospitalization were voluntary.

State officials wouldn't reveal the timing or circum-

stances of Nau's release from the hospital. But one official implied that Nau left because medical staff found no legal ground to hold him against his will.

Jack Bardeson, deputy director of the Division of Mental Health, said that, in general, the release of a voluntary mental patient implies a staff decision "that the situation didn't warrant using the law to hold" him.

Voluntary mental patients can end their treatment at any time unless they are found to be mentally disabled or a danger to themselves or others, Bardeson said.

The (research) literature says that prediction of violence is a very underdeveloped art," he added.

In the past two years, Nau was treated at the Veterans Administration Medical Center in Denver for mental illness, according to a source who asked not to be identified. A medical center official confirmed that Nau had been a patient there.

But Nau rejected his parents' suggestions to return there Sept. 24 after he threatened his brothers, prompting his parents to call police, Rupp said.

The Naus Friday declined to speak with the News.

Nau received treatment, including medication, while in the Navy, according to Rupp. He was honorably discharged in November 1981.

Nau isn't the first mental patient in the Denver area to kill someone soon after release from a public mental institution. At least two other cases have occurred in the last four years.

In 1980, Andrew McCoy stabbed to death a stranger at Stapleton International Airport, just weeks after his release from Fort Logan Mental Health Center in Denver. A lawsuit brought by the victim's family against the center was settled out of court for $21,500.

Friends baffled by slayings in close-knit family

By ARNOLD LEVINSON and JANE HULSE
Rocky Mountain News Staff Writers

LITTLETON — A gunshot downstairs woke Debbie Nau from an afternoon nap. She called police.

Within minutes, another shot was fired next door, where Carol Mason was on the phone with police.

Two shots, two brothers dead — allegedly slain by another brother.

Friends, neighbors and police said Friday they are trying to understand what happened in a family filled with love.

"It's really a mess," Detective Dan Rupp said as he studied accounts of events on Thursday.

Mason, a neighbor, and her brother, Jeff, told the Rocky Mountain News they were in their kitchen when Bruce Nau, 20, rang the doorbell. Carol answered, and Bruce burst into the house, saying his brother Richard

had shot their brother James.

Bruce dashed down to the basement. Carol was on the phone with Littleton police when Richard Nau, 22, entered with a rifle. He followed his brother downstairs, and the two argued briefly before Carol heard a gunshot.

When Richard Nau came back upstairs, he told Jeff Mason to "leave him alone" and walked out of the house, Mason said.

James Nau, 32, died in the Nau family home.

"He loved his brother (Richard) very much." said a family friend who asked not to be identified. The friend said the Nau family of six brothers and two sisters had no history of animosity.

"They were a very close family," the friend said. "There was a lot of love in that group."

James returned last year to the home at 746 W.

Peakview Ave. after spending a year working on a shrimp boat in Alaska, the friend said. He was an adventurous man who liked to travel and climb the icy Rockies in winter.

"He loved the mountains," the friend said.

Friday morning, Richard Nau was advised of his rights in Arapahoe County Court, then returned to Arapahoe County Jail where he is being held without bond. He is scheduled to appear in court Oct. 5 for formal filing of charges.

Seven years ago, he was named All-Metro bantam goalie in an industrial hockey league. As a freshman hockey player for Heritage High School, he told the News in 1977:

"I don't like to get scored on . . . Nobody has run the score up on me. They can't."

Case ends quickly, Nau confined in state hospital

By Shirley Smith
Sentinel Writer

The law moved swiftly in the case of Richard Nau, 22, accused of the murder of his brothers, Bruce, 20, and James, 32, Sept. 29.

Nau was whisked to the state mental hospital the day after he pleaded not guilty by reason of insanity at a hearing Oct. 5 in Littleton District Court, according to Arapahoe County Sheriff Pat Sullivan.

Sullivan said he was surprised at the speed the case was settled.

"A preliminary hearing is a test for cause for a trial, but a plea can be taken," he said. "Two doctors testified as to his insanity. The district attorney as well as Nau's attorney agreed to wrap it up."

The murder of the Nau's brothers occurred after a desperate attempt by the Nau family to get psychiatric help for Richard. Just a few days before the tragedy Nau committed himself voluntarily to the state hospital in Pueblo after an evaluation by Arapahoe Mental Health, but he did not stay.

His father, Gerald Nau, said Nau's problems began while he was in the Navy. The young man spent time in the Veterans Hospital, but would not take the necessary medication after he left. Although the family tried to get a court order for Richard to take the medication, the judge refused the request.

Sullivan said that while Richard was in the Arapahoe County Jail he claimed to see scorpions on the wall, and thought the staff was putting things in his food. He was held in

an isolation cell.

Sullivan said he suspected Nau would be in the state mental institution at least two or three years before he could petition the court for a sanity hearing. Sullivan said his stay there would be indefinite.

ALTHOUGH THE MURDERS occurred in Littleton, the sheriff's department was called in the afternoon of the deaths to evacuate Euclid Junior High. The Nau home is next door. Nau was not apprehended by the Cherry Hills police until later in the day.

Sullivan said when the call came he rushed to Euclid where his daughter is a student.

"We cleared the classrooms on the level facing the Nau back yard. Teachers grabbed groups," Sullivan said. He said principal Vern Harder and assistant principal Flo Bullock were kept busy and the operation went smoothly. No one panicked.

Sullivan is a neighbor of the Naus, and attends the same church. He knew Bruce Nau well. He termed the event "a tragedy."

Birth forum slated

A forum on many aspects of birth will be presented Saturday from 9 a.m. to 4:30 p.m. at the Marriott Hotel, Interstate 25 and East Hampden Avenue. Phone 466-7965 for reservations.

Slayer of Brothers Is Found Insane

By BILL McBEAN
Denver Post Staff Writer

Six days after he shot and killed his two brothers, Richard Jay Nau Thursday was committed to the Colorado State Hospital by a Littleton District Court judge who found him not guilty of the deaths by reason of insanity.

The speedy resolution of Nau's case resulted from a rare cooperative effort between Arapahoe County District Attorney Bob Gallagher and Craig Truman, head of the Littleton public defender's office, who used the case to publicly condemn Colorado's mental health services.

It was Judge Charles Friedman — after a 1½ hour combination preliminary and sanity hearing — who sent the 22-year-old Nau to the state hospital for an undetermined period of treatment.

Nau had been released from the state hospital just two days before he found his father's hidden deer rifle a week ago today and shot his brothers — 20-year-old Bruce Nau and 32-year-old Jim Nau — to death.

In a press conference after the hearing, Gallagher and Truman revealed that Nau was released from the state hospital because the Arapahoe Mental Health Center insisted he didn't need to be hospital-

Nau committed to state hospital.

ized.

"I find that incredible," Gallagher said.

However, the district attorney said he wasn't looking for someone

Please See NAU on 14-A

Brothers' killer ruled innocent by insanity

Mental-health system decried

By JANE HULSE
Rocky Mountain News Staff Writer

LITTLETON — Richard Nau, who killed his two brothers in a delusional rage Sept. 29 two days after his release from the state mental hospital, was ruled innocent by reason of insanity Wednesday in the double homicide.

The senseless killings sparked mutual outrage from Nau's attorney, Craig Truman, and District Attorney Robert Gallagher, who criticized state mental health officials for letting loose potentially dangerous mental patients.

"Why does it take two deaths to get this guy [Nau] the help he so desperately needed?" Gallagher asked Wednesday after District Judge Charles Friedman's ruling.

The judge ordered Nau, 22, to the State Hospital in Pueblo for treatment for an indefinite period of time. During the hearing two psychiatrists testified that Nau thought his brothers were possessed by malicious spirits and that he was saving the "universe" by shooting them. He still feels the act was "justified," one doctor said.

Two psychiatrists testified Wednesday that Nau suffered from chronic paranoid schizophrenia. They said his mental problems surfaced while he served in the Navy 2½ years ago. He heard voices, believed he was being followed, and at times thought he was Jesus Christ or God. He was tormented by struggles between good and evil.

Despite frequent hospitalizations, his mental condition deteriorated, they said. He believed he was turning into a black person, thought his brother was poisoning his food, and believed that family members had been replaced by stand-ins.

One doctor who examined him this week

said that Nau originally wanted to plead self-defense for the two killings. He said Nau pointed to his chest, complained that it was caved in, and contended one of his brothers had taken out his soul.

Gallagher said that Nau has had a histo-

ry of chronic mental illness for 2½ years, yet two days after he was admitted to the state hospital for making delusional threats against family members, he was released.

"I'm angry and I'm worried," said Tru-

man, who represented the slight, boyish-looking Nau at a sanity hearing Wednesday.

"I don't know who dropped the ball," t

See BROTHER, page

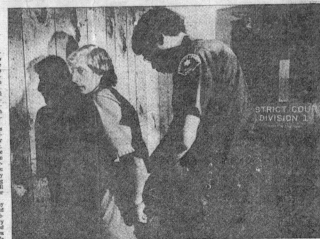

Charley Nau is handcuffed outside District Court before he is returned to his cell in Littleton.

Slayer of Brothers Sent to Hospital

NAU From 1-A

to blame for the deaths.

"I'm not so much concerned with who dropped the ball in this case," Gallagher said. "I'm concerned with who drops the ball all the time."

During the press conference, the prosecutor and defense attorney questioned how many more innocent people would have to die at the hands of mentally ill individuals who couldn't get the help they needed.

Truman, who has been defending accused murderers in Colorado for more than 10 years, said there have been five or six cases of mentally ill people committing homicides in Colorado in the last few years.

People needing treatment "get worse and worse until someone dies," Truman said. "They have to kill people to get the mental health treatment they need."

Gallagher also said that in July Nau was in the Denver Veteran's Administration Hospital on a 180-day mental health hold when he walked away from the facility. Gallagher said the VA reacted by giving his bed to another patient and withdrawing Nau's certification of mental illness.

Gallagher and Truman challenged the Colorado Legislature to appoint a panel to examine the state's mental health delivery systems, obtain information from other states and then institute the necessary reforms.

The Veterans' Administration couldn't be reached for comment on Gallagher's remarks.

Thomas Machiorletti, executive director of the Arapahoe Mental Health Center, declined to discuss the Nau case but did defend the

The Denver Post / Dennis Chamberlin
Littleton Public Defender Truman, center, and Arapahoe District Attorney Gallagher speak with reporters.

Legislature's track record on mental health problems.

The state fiscal situation, Machiorletti said, means that everyone must expect budget cuts. The Legislature has "treated the mental health system reasonably well," he said.

However, Machiorletti confirmed the Colorado State Hospital has only 15 beds reserved for residents of Arapahoe County.

During Nau's court hearing, two psychiatrists testified that they be-

lieved Nau was legally insane when he shot his brothers.

Both Dr. John Macdonald of the University of Colorado Health Sciences Center and Dr. Seymour Sundell, who works for Denver, agreed that Nau is a chronic paranoid schizophrenic who needs to take anti-psychotic medication over a long period of time.

Macdonald testified that Nau thought he was God and Jesus Christ and that he had a mission to free the earth from evil.

Both psychiatrists said Nau believed evil spirits had taken over his brothers, that his brothers were not their real selves but "replacements."

"To this date, even after the fact, he feels his act was justified," Sundell said.

Nau felt he was "one of God's knights," Sundell said. He quoted Nau as saying of one of his brothers, "He may be my brother in appearance, but he's really Jack the Ripper."

Suspect in Slayings Of Kin Reportedly Threatened Family

By BILL McBEAN
Denver Post Staff Writer

Richard Jay Nau threatened his family and his therapist with death on several occasions in the months before he allegedly shot his two brothers to death, but neither the Colorado State Hospital nor the Veterans Administration Hospital diagnosed him as dangerous, according to sources close to the case.

The Denver Post has learned that the 22-year-old Nau threatened to kill members of his Littleton family with a gun he purchased last April. Nau's father confiscated the gun and returned it to the store where his son had bought it.

Last Thursday, Jim Nau, 32, and Bruce Nau, 20, were wounded fatally — one in the Nau family home and the other at a house down the street. The weapon used was a deer rifle belonging to Nau's father that had been hidden in the elder Nau's bedroom.

Their brother, Richard, is being held at the Arapahoe County Jail, without bond, in connection with the slayings. Last summer, during a stay at the Veterans Administration Hospital in Denver, Nau theatened to kill his therapist and also said he would have his therapist's home burglarized, according to sources close to the case.

On another occasion, when Nau's parents were admitting him to the same hospital, he bolted. When his father and two guards tried to restrain him, he fought back with his fists and feet.

Please See NAU on 6-A

Sources Report Case History Of Threats by Slaying Suspect

NAU From 1-A

Officials at the VA Hospital determined they couldn't make any progress in curing Nau's paranoid-schizophrenic mental condition unless hospital officials could force him to take anti-psychotic medication.

However, Littleton District Chief Judge Robert Kelley, after a hearing last July, refused to give the VA permission to force Nau to take the drugs.

Kelley is on vacation and couldn't be reached for comment. Authorities Monday refused to release Kelley's written legal opinion on the case, but sources said that opinion will be released soon, probably today.

On Aug. 10, after the District Court hearing, Nau escaped from the VA Hospital. Although they later learned where he was staying, federal officials gave his bed to another patient and determined Nau wasn't a danger to the community. They gave him no medication and there was no further follow-up, sources said.

Nau was to have started vocational training at the Denver Federal Center, but by Aug. 24 he was in the Colorado State Hospital in Pueblo where he was diagnosed as a chronic paranoid schizophrenic.

However, the doctor who examined Nau, Steven D. Dworetsky, determined Nau was neither suicidal nor homicidal and would be a good outpatient candidate in the Arapahoe Mental Health Center's halfway house. Nau was released three days after he had been transported to Pueblo by ambulance.

Dworetsky, contacted late Monday, refused to comment on the case. However, sources said the state hospital didn't have Nau's files from the Veterans Administration and apparently didn't know of Nau's propensity for violence.

If the courts determine that Nau is the killer of his brothers, the tragedy would be another in a series of cases where mental health officials have released potentially dangerous patients who later were arrested in connection with killings.

The Denver suburban Southwest Mental Health Center came under fire in late 1979, for example, after it allowed David Delacruz to remain free. He later stabbed an RTD bus driver to death.

Seth Andrew Buckmaster of Denver shot a Colorado Springs police officer to death in April 1980. He had been released earlier from Denver's Fort Logan Mental Health Center.

In February 1980, Andrew McCoy Jr. stabbed an unsuspecting stranger to death while standing in a ticket line at Stapleton International Airport. McCoy also was a former Fort Logan patient.

State doctors fear Nau still dangerous

By Linda Dowlen Roberts

LITTLETON — Psychiatrists treating a Littleton man committed to a state hospital for the murder of his two brothers are requesting a court order forcing him to take antipsychotic medication because they fear he may attempt another homicide.

Richard J. Nau, 746 W. Peakview Ave., was diagnosed as a chronic paranoic schizophrenic and committed Oct. 6 to the Institute for Forensic Psychology at the Colorado State Hospital. He had been released from the state hospital two days before he used his father's deer rifle Sept. 29 to shoot his 20-year-old brother, Bruce, and 32-year-old brother, Jim.

A visiting court judge in Littleton District Court is scheduled to hear the matter Monday.

A June 8 report from treating psychiatrist Alan S. Fine states he "feels Nau is acutely homicidal and plans to murder someone on this ward."

Nau has refused to take antipsychotic medication but has been having delusions that people were out to kill him, Fine said.

Nau has also told doctors he has been hearing voices telling him he was doomed and that he needs to pray for his salvation. He thinks people are sucking air out of him at night and on one occasion got up in the middle of the night and put his hands around another patient's throat, the psychiatrist said.

Staff members also caught Nau trying to steal a piece of silverware that they thought could be a potential weapon.

Nau is presently in seclusion, wearing physical restraints, but doctors wish to administer the drug Haldol in order to allow him back on the ward without being a danger to others, Fine said.

Nau's case has been turned over to Dr. Robert Huffaker who is expected to testify Monday.

Court orders Nau to take his medicine

By Linda Dowlen Roberts

LITTLETON — It was a quiet and coherent Richard J. Nau who spoke in Littleton District Court Monday, requesting that he not be forced to take medication at the Colorado State Hospital in Pueblo.

But although noting Nau's concerns, Judge Marvin Foote ordered that the state hospital be allowed to force Nau to take his medication if he did not do so voluntarily. The court added that the order would be reviewed in January.

Nau, 22, was committed to the hospital in October after being found not guilty by reason of insanity for the shooting deaths of his two brothers, Bruce, 20, and James, 32.

When he was first brought to the hospital, he was "very psychotic, very delusional," said Dr. Robert Huffaker, the state hospital's chief of psychiatry. Recently, doctors have been concerned about the safety of the staff and patients at the hospital because Nau has been "engaging in bizarre activities" such as praying in the middle of the dining room, talking about people hurting him and being found in the middle of the night with his hands around another patient's throat, he said.

But yesterday, his hands cuffed to a leather belt at his waist, Nau told the court he feared taking antipsychotic drugs because "in a closed environment it increases your paranoia and makes you feel very bad."

"I think the doctor is really going to abuse the medication on me and give it in high dosages," he said. "I have my problems, I know that. . .I don't want to go insane. . .but (taking medication) is my personal right."

State gets OK to treat Nau against his will

By KIT MINICLIER
Denver Post Staff Writer

LITTLETON — His legs in irons, his hands cuffed and manacled to a thick leather belt, Richard Jay Nau testified under oath Monday that he killed his brother James "because he was trying to suck the spirit out of me."

"I wished I didn't shoot him, but I did," Nau said, adding that James "was definitely a devil worshiper."

Nau, 22, was found innocent by reason of insanity last October in the Sept. 29 killings of his brothers Bruce, 20, and James, 32, only two days after he was released from the state mental hospital.

He was in Littleton District Court Monday to protest a state request for permission to medicate him against his will, if necessary. His protests failed.

"I did take some extreme action," Nau said of James' death, adding: "I don't think I'd do that again because I've learned that crime doesn't pay."

Paul King, a deputy Arapahoe County district attorney, asked Nau if he had tried to talk to James. He replied: "I did, but it didn't do any good."

Nau, who remained in restraints and under guard by two deputies during his 18 minutes of testimony, spoke clearly and responded quickly to questions by King and his attorney, Public Defender Craig Truman.

Asked why he didn't always agree to take medication, Nau, attired in a yellow 1980 World's Fair T-shirt and burgundy slacks, replied:

"In a closed environment it increases paranoia and makes you feel bad ... I know when I need medication and I know when I don't."

Nau told presiding Judge Marvin Foote that he was treated "like an animal" at the state mental hospital. He asked to go home or to a Veterans Administration hospital, explaining "I'm a veteran, your honor."

Dr. Robert Huffaker, a psychiatrist at the state hospital, testified that a court order permitting forceful medication is needed because Nau sometimes refuses to

Nau was manacled for hearing.

woke to find Nau standing over him, saying "someone will have to die," Huffaker said. Another patient said he woke to find Nau's hands around his neck.

"Our whole eight-month hospitalization has been a constant struggle to get him to take his medication," Huffaker said, explaining that last December the hospital dropped legal efforts to get a medication order because Nau agreed to take his drugs.

Asking the court "for permission to treat him against his will," Huffaker said Nau would be restrained and given medication by injection, if he refused to swallow his drugs.

The doctor said there are about 10 different anti-psychotic drugs, which are given on a "trial and error" basis "to see what hurts the person the least."

Nau said other patients tried to put a hex on him and "I hear God talking to me. He says, 'Believe in Me.'" He doesn't hear witches voices anymore, he added.

Conceding the danger of side effects, King told the judge "two people are dead as a result of Mr. Nau's illness. We can't afford a third or fourth."

Nau told the judge "I definitely won't take the medication all the time."

Foote commended Nau for his "clear, lucid" testimony, but granted the state's request in the interest of Nau's treatment and "to protect the public interest."

Foote said medication may be

Richard Jay Nau killed his two brothers, James and Bruce, left.

On a morning in late September this year, Richard Jay Nau of Littleton told his mother he saw demons coming out of the walls of their home and scorpions moving around her.

The hallucinations of demons, scorpions and the devil seethed in Nau's mind during the two months he had gone without the medication psychiatrists said was necessary to treat and control his mental illness.

On the afternoon of Sept. 29, Nau went to his parents' bedroom and took his father's .300-caliber savage rifle from its hiding place.

Convinced that evil spirits had taken over his two brothers, Nau then fatally shot his brother, Jim, 22. At a neighbor's home, Nau tracked down and killed his brother, Bruce, 20.

Within a week of the slayings, Nau was found insane in a Littleton court and was committed for an indefinite period of treatment to the Colorado State Hospital, where he remains in the maximum-security unit.

Paranoid schizophrenia was the diagnosis for Nau after he was discharged from the Navy in 1981 because of extreme distress. Doctors made that same diagnosis when Nau was hospitalized three times at the Veterans Administration Medical Center in Denver and twice at two other psychiatric facilities in the Denver area over a 20-month period ending last July.

When psychiatrists at the Veterans Administration facility went to court in July to force Nau to take his medications there, they said the medication was necessary because Nau — then a patient on a 90-day mental-health hold at the center — was potentially dangerous to himself and to others.

But Littleton District Judge Robert Kelley ruled that Nau, 22, couldn't be tied down and forced to take medication that Nau said made his brain "feel like a rock" and caused deterioration of his eyesight.

There are other "less intrusive" means of treating Nau at the hospital, such as group therapy or individual therapy, Kelley

ruled. However, Kelley did acknowledge that Nau was mentally ill, needed to be hospitalized and was a danger to himself and his family.

Shortly after the ruling, Nau walked away from the medical center and returned home. And center officials declined to provide Nau's family with medication that Nau might — or might not — take at home.

The next day, Nau's bed at the center was given to another patient.

Informing the judge of Nau's early discharge, center officials said Nau "had shown an increased ability to make reasonable plans for himself," and "he is not considered an imminent danger to himself or others at this time" — a conclusion differing markedly from the same officials' statement given to the court just a few weeks earlier.

Less than a week before Nau killed his two brothers, he had been taken to the State Hospital after threatening members of his family. But hospital officials didn't request Nau's records from the Veterans

CHAPTER TEN

Sadness Flies Away on the Wings of Time

It has been thirty years since Jim and Bruce died. My family has come a long way during those years. It took us many years of grieving to overcome our feelings of depression and sadness over this terrible tragedy. It was difficult for me to see each family member deal with individual pain caused from the experience. However, we made it through. This story is not just about schizophrenia, it is also about the survival of a family. It is about love of a son and love of a sibling who fought an incurable brain disease.

For twenty-six years, Ricky lived in the Colorado State Mental Institution in Pueblo, Colorado. He had a very difficult journey. For the first few years he was in maximum security, which means when we went to visit we had to do a full-body search to get in, and we had to go through a lot of heavily secured doors. The maximum-security floor housed the most sick and dangerous individuals. Most had committed murder or other very serious crimes.

When we went to visit Ricky, we were always led to a large room where guards, attendants and counselors watched the visit.

Plus, there were usually other inmates visiting their families too. It was nerve-racking to see Ricky in this environment. It was a sad, cold and lonely place. I was not scared to see Ricky; however, I was a little scared of the other inmates. They made me nervous because of the way they looked at me. They were always staring and making odd expressions. I almost felt like at any moment they would jump at or attack me.

The visitations with Ricky during this time were hard. Sometimes I would bring up the topic of Jim and Bruce. Ricky would either believe they were not dead, shut down, withdraw or became deeply depressed. He never discussed the topic because he had a very difficult time accepting it. He would rather push it back in his heart and mind and avoid it at all costs.

Only one time in those twenty-six years did Ricky mention that day. He said to me out of the blue, "I'm glad that I wasn't able to get into your bedroom because I would have killed you." Chills prickled down my spine when he said that to me. I know in his heart it was his way of apologizing and letting me know that he was glad I was alive. I tried to make light of the situation and told him in a joking manner with a smile on my face, "Well, I'm sure glad you didn't get into my room, too!" It seemed to release the tension — and it was my way of telling him it was okay.

Ricky had to try a few different medications to find the one that best suited him. There were not that many choices of medications thirty years ago, and most had terrible side effects. Sometimes Ricky was in a daze or coma like state. Sometimes he would stare and his eyes would have a glazed look. He would get extreme dry mouth, itch or twitch, act extremely nervous, still hear voices or see things, and still act paranoid. He would not eat salt or other food items because he thought it would bring demons into his room or his body.

Over time, the medications improved greatly. Ricky started to progress and get better. For quite a few years, he was in medium security, which allowed more freedom. He would participate in art or woodworking classes and other activities. Once he started doing activities, you could see a change in his personality. He was more vibrant and excited about life in general.

Many times over the years, Ricky tried to go to court to get released from the hospital. The court system and the judge always read his reports and the doctor's notes. Thank goodness, they never considered releasing him. I felt it was a good decision from the judge — I don't believe in my heart he would have been able to survive society, daily living, and the responsibilities that go with it. Plus, I know Ricky would have stopped taking his medication. He still did not believe in his mind that he needed it. The hospital always had to watch him very closely to make sure he took his medication. If he did stop, he would be back to serious hallucinations, paranoia, and violent outburst.

Over the years when Ricky was in medium security, more medications came onto the market. There were a couple types of medications that he tried that did pretty well for him. Once that happened, he progressed to minimum security. This type of security allowed Ricky to play basketball or swim. He also got to go outside and walk around the grounds.

These visits were a lot more comfortable and fun. We played board games or a game of pool. The hospital allowed us to bring food from Arby's, McDonalds or whatever Ricky was hungry for. He had become more enjoyable to be around. I also noticed he started to develop friendships with other inmates.

The conversations with Ricky were becoming more fulfilling. We spoke of football, hockey, baseball, movies and whatever topics that were headline news for the day. I remember one time when I

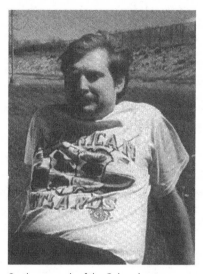

On the grounds of the Colorado
State Hospital
The day I had the picnic with Ricky

was visiting Ricky, he was really excited to show me around the hospital grounds. My parents went outside to set up a table for a picnic lunch while he and I took a walk. It was a beautiful sunny day, and it was such a nice feeling to be alone with him without being scared. We laughed and joked and for a few minutes I saw a glimpse of the old Ricky. Our visit only lasted for a short time; however, that short time was a special moment I will never forget.

Over the last several years, Ricky had been doing great! He started to develop a comfort level with the hospital and he had no desire to be free. I think he became scared of society and finally accepted that the hospital was his home. He seemed happy and relaxed.

The hospital staff would take him off the grounds to go swimming, see movies or watch baseball games. Whenever I visited him, we often played card games and enjoyed pleasant conversations. He was taking a really good medication that did wonders for him. He started working a part-time job off hospital grounds at a computer company and did quite well for himself. If you had met him, you would have never known he was sick. He seemed completely normal. I became proud and happy for him because he finally came to a place where he forgave himself for what he did to Jim and Bruce. The guilt and pain he must have carried was incomprehensible. It took him many years to open up and talk to his counselor about the situation. He finally got to a great place in his life.

Ricky gave my mom an unexpected gift. The first weekend of January 2009 my mom, dad and brother Gene went down to Pueblo to visit Ricky. During their visit, when they were playing games, Ricky looked at my mom and stated in a sweet, gentle voice, "In case I don't get another chance, I wanted you to know that everything that happened was not your fault! You were a good mom, and I love you."

"Thank you, Rick, that meant a lot to me," she said as tears rolled down her face while she grabbed his hand and squeezed it. All the guilt she felt over the years wondering if she did enough for him or was a good enough mom was finally released.

Ricky then turned to my dad and said with deep gratitude, "Thank you for coming to see me every month and supporting me all these years."

"You're welcome, Rick," my dad said as he grabbed Ricky's shoulder and squeezed it. I know that meant a lot to Dad, too. Ricky had never said anything like that to my parents before.

Unfortunately, Ricky passed away a week later on Monday, January 12, 2009 from a blood clot to the heart. It was unexpected and a shock.

Based on what he said to my parents, I do not know if he knew he was going to die or if he was concerned my mom was going to die because she was battling ovarian cancer. We found out after the fact that Ricky had been struggling with his own health issues for a few months prior to his death. He had loss of breath and heart pains. Ricky had instructed the hospital not to tell my parents because he did not want to worry them.

So when he did pass away, it was a complete surprise. I was deeply saddened that I did not get a chance to see him before he died. The last time I saw him was nine months prior for his birthday. I always visited him at Christmas, but the weather conditions were bad that year, and I didn't get a chance to visit him. I do feel a sense of guilt over that; however, it gives me great comfort to know he is now free from this horrible disease. He is with God, Jim and Bruce.

Still, to this day, I often think about Ricky and his life's journey. I believe with all my heart that the drugs he did trigger his schizophrenia. It is hard to comprehend his illness and what he went through physically, mentally and emotionally. None of us really have any idea what it is like to be schizophrenic. The hallucinations schizophrenics see and hear (monsters and voices) are beyond our comprehension and understanding. The guilt and sadness he endured knowing what he did must have been unbearable. I am so glad and proud that my family and I never turned our backs on him. He needed our love and support to live though his illness and make peace with his journey.

As for my parents, the pain that they suffered over the last thirty years I don't think anyone would understand until they become a parent and lose a child. As a parent, you always feel it is your job to take care of your children, to protect them, to help them, and to guide them. When something goes terribly wrong or out of your control, and you're not able to provide these things for your children anymore, it causes a lot of guilt and frustration. The guilt my parents endured was very difficult for them. They felt guilt for not protecting Jim and Bruce; they felt guilt for not helping Ricky enough; they felt guilt for not protecting the rest of us kids from the pain of death; and they felt guilt for living longer than their own children. It definitely took an emotional toll on Mom and Dad, but they always managed to work through it and stay strong in their faith, religion and marriage.

Not only did my parents have to deal with guilt, but also they dealt with mourning the loss of three children, Jim and Bruce to death, and Ricky to mental illness. Although Ricky was alive, after he became sick, he was never the child they knew and loved. So, those feelings of loss are similar to the feelings of death — basically a death of something they knew that was no more.

My parents experienced myriad emotions, shock, sadness, depression, guilt, acceptance, frustration, anger, love and happiness over the years. It truly makes them amazing in my eyes. Even though they were going through their own pain, they never put themselves or their grieving process ahead of their children. They always put their children's needs first, no matter what, and their own needs second. My parents continued support of all of us kids over the years was honorable. They were there when we needed them or needed help. My siblings and I could always count on their loyalty and love.

During those twenty-six years with Ricky, my parents visited him every month. I am not exaggerating! They drove down to Pueblo to see him the second Saturday of every single month. The only time they didn't visit him was if there was a terrible snowstorm and road conditions were bad or if they were really sick with the flu. Even then, they would try to go the following weekend to make up for the missed visits.

They were completely loyal to Ricky and never abandoned him at any point in time. To me, that shows great love, compassion, forgiveness and most importantly, a loving,

Mom and Dad
50th Wedding Anniversary photo

committed parent and Christian. Their actions taught me a lot about being a good person, forgiving others, and putting someone else's needs ahead of my own. I'm proud of my parents for what they went through, how they managed to stay together through difficult times; and most importantly, how they never gave up on their child because he was sick. They loved Ricky unconditionally no matter what he did. They were truly amazing!

Over several years, my mom battled ovarian cancer. There were a couple of times she had to miss visiting Ricky due to the illness associated with chemo. Mom and I would have discussions about Ricky and who would take care of him after my parents passed away. I had to reassure Mom that we would not abandon Ricky and would be there for him. I think when he passed away, it gave my mom a sense of relief knowing she did not have to task her surviving children with taking care of him. She felt that Ricky had put us through enough in our lives; we should not have to watch over him, too. I thought that was silly of her to think that. Family is family. You don't abandon them because they're sick.

Unfortunately, my mom passed away in June 2010 from ovarian cancer. She had a three-year battle she could no longer fight. Bless her heart. I was a very lucky girl. I had a great mom who supported me in everything I did. She understood the vision I had in writing this book and hopefully helping other families. We talked and dreamed about helping the mentally ill and starting a charity fund.

The day of my mom's burial, my husband and I showed up to the cemetery early. Mom was going to be buried in the same plot as my brother Bruce. This is a military cemetery; children and wife can be buried in the same plot as the husband. Because Bruce died before the age of twenty-one, he was buried in my dad's plot. Now my mom was going to join him. Jim was buried next to them, and Ricky was buried a hundred yards away.

Out of a morbid curiosity, I went over to the plot where my mom would be lowered. I looked down the hole to see if I could see Bruce's coffin. There was only dirt. I'm not sure why, but I felt such a need to see his coffin, I guess to remind myself that it all really did happen. I don't know. I guess I missed him and needed some type of connection again. As we stood there, Jim's headstone was moved to the side to make room for the burial. Each headstone has a number assigned to it because it's a military cemetery. Jim's number is 1464.

My husband and I had a little extra time before the service started, so we went over to visit Ricky's gravesite. As I stood there saying a few prayers, my husband walked around Ricky's headstone and noticed the numbers were similar to Jim's. Ricky's numbers were 4641. What? How could that be? We drove back over to Jim's gravesite to verify. Sure enough, Ricky's number was a *mirror* image of Jim's! I cannot believe none of us noticed the same numbers until that day.

Ricky was buried twenty-six years after Jim. What are the odds of that? Thousands of people have been buried at this cemetery since Jim, and now, they both have the same numbers! Is that not a "wink" from God? To me, He was saying it was all meant to be,

Jim's Headstone
1464

Ricky's Headstone
4641

and they are all together. I thought it was truly amazing!

As for my siblings, they are all doing great. My brother Gene received his Ph.D. from the University of Tennessee in biology and has been a research scientist for many years. He now dedicates his life to teaching college students and is currently a lecturer at a local private university. Gene is also currently working on several books, one of which is about the neurophysiology of addictive behavior and the other is about the role of plant alkaloids in arthritis. My sister Theresa has two beautiful daughters and three grandchildren. She has a Certified Payroll Professional degree and works for a local company. My brother Jeff has a wonderful daughter and grandson. He received his Airframe and Power Plant License from Colorado Aero Tech. He has spent many years maintaining helicopters in various parts of the world. Recently, he was awarded his first U.S. patent for an Electromagnetic Vertical Flight Propulsion Device (that's all he will let me say). Finally, my brother Charlie has two fantastic sons and a gorgeous daughter. He received an Electronic Engineering Technology degree from ITT Technical Institute and works for a local firm.

I am so proud of all my brothers and my sister because they have all been successful in their own right. However, in the beginning, they all went through difficulties in dealing with the loss of Jim and Bruce. Each of them mourned in their own way. To be honest with you, I still feel that they have not completely healed from this tragedy. I think the memories are embedded in the back of their minds and plays into their lives more than they realize and understand. I know they were all very hurt when this happened, and they all had a hard time understanding why. Each of my brothers had wonderful qualities we all love and miss. It has taken many years for my siblings to get to a good place in their lives.

They have all shown great character and qualities during the difficult times, and they never turned their backs on Ricky. I know there were times they were embarrassed about Ricky and what he did, and there were times when they were very angry. I also know there were times when some of my siblings experienced rude and negative comments from acquaintances or old friends about Ricky and what he did.

Still today, it is *shocking* for me to hear that someone could be so ignorant, cruel and mean as to pass judgment on an innocent family that experienced a horrible tragedy and a sibling who was desperately sick. I told my siblings, it's times like that when you have to stand tall and be proud of your family's name because it's the negative situations that builds character and helps you grow personally and spiritually. You can never let someone else's stupidity about mental illness bring you down.

When all was said and done, my family has stuck together through all the good and bad times, and they have always loved and supported Ricky. I could not have asked for anything more

First family picture after Jim and Bruce died
It took ten years for us to be able to take this picture without them.
Top L to R: Dad, Mom
Bottom L to R: Jeff, Theresa, Debbie, Gene, Charlie

from God than that — to keep my family together. A tragedy like this can easily tear any family apart. It has been a hard road for everyone, but we stick it out every day, work hard, enjoy our families, and keep living and moving forward in a positive way because that's what Jim, Bruce and Ricky would have wanted.

CHAPTER ELEVEN

As One Learns to Fly, One Becomes Free

A s for me, the journey has been long. The grief process was hard and took me over fifteen years to work through. I felt a great deal of pain from the way some friends treated me. I had to put my feelings aside to finish high school. It took a lot of courage and strength to focus on homework and be a teenager again. I wanted to fit in so badly, but I never felt like I did. I felt like a loner.

There were many times when I was walking down the hall in high school and I could hear whispers of people saying, "That's the girl with the brother who is a murderer." I had to hold my tears in and keep my head held high. I could not let them see my pain. Unfortunately, kids can be cruel. My friends were too immature to handle the intense emotional feelings and situation I was dealing with. There was no way a seventeen or eighteen year old could empathize with those feelings. So at first, I had a really hard time. I felt very alone… again.

Many of my friends over the years asked me if I hated Ricky for what he did, and my response was: "No! I never hated Ricky — and I never will." I remember the looks on their faces of surprise or shock as they asked, "How could you not hate him? What is wrong with you? After what he did to your family?"

I tried to explain. I had such feelings of love and compassion for him that hate was not even considered. I asked my friends, how could you stop loving someone just because they are mentally ill? Would you stop loving someone because they have cancer? Would you stop loving someone because they have multiple sclerosis? No! It's a disease just like schizophrenia. It was the mental illness that caused this tragedy, not Ricky as a true soul. They were shocked at my response — and they never asked again.

During my college years, I had a lot of really nice friends and overall had a pretty good time. There were times I partied hard and drank heavily to forget the pain and memories, but they would always reappear in the back of my mind the next day.

For the first two years of college, I continuously and obsessively cut my hair out of survivor's guilt. I felt guilty for surviving instead of Jim and Bruce. I felt guilty for not being able to stop Ricky. Maybe if I had grabbed the gun instead of calling the police, Bruce would still be alive today. I felt guilty for not being able to help Ricky and my parents. I took my anger out on myself by cutting my hair, feeling that no one would see my pain if I looked plain and ugly. Furthermore, it was the only thing I felt I could control. My life was difficult, and I felt like I had no sense of balance or control. It seemed like my life was in everyone else's hands.

Finally, my family home life was depressing, and I fell into the role of being the caretaker. I was too busy trying to help my family that I could not help myself. After a couple of years of depression and not being able to sleep, I decided to take anti-depressive medication to help me feel better. I took the medication for a year. It did help overall, but in reality, nothing can ever take away those memories.

All through college, my family and I pursued a lawsuit against the Colorado State Hospital and the Veterans Administration (hospital), and I was the main component. It was very stressful to deal with all the lawyers, doctors, depositions and memories of details of what happened that day while trying to study for school. Every time I started to feel good and happy again, I would get dragged back to Denver to discuss with the lawyer some detail of that day. It kept making me revisit the pain and ruined my attempts at happiness.

The lawsuit settled the night before our court date. Unfortunately, due to the nature of the agreement, I cannot say the names of the doctors or disclose the settlement amount even though I want to. I feel the doctors' names should be told so they can take responsibility for their lack of professionalism and utter unwillingness to help Ricky or my family.

The only thing I can say is, the lawsuit did bring some closure. We did prove that the hospitals and doctors were negligent for their actions. We also stood up for Jim and Bruce's memories.

Furthermore, my family had made an effort to bring some type of justice to this terrible tragedy.

And life went on…

I graduated from college with a Bachelor of Arts in Psychology with a minor in Criminal Law. I pursued this degree because of Jim, Bruce and Ricky. I wanted to understand mental illness, and how it all pertains to the law. I also wanted to help troubled

My Graduation
University of Northern Colorado

kids and teenagers, to hopefully prevent them from going down the path of using drugs, which could eventually lead them to a fate like Ricky's. I thought maybe I could prevent that road from being taken.

This desire, while honorable, just wasn't a good choice for me — especially coming off so many raw and painful feelings that I was just starting to resolve. During my internship at a detox center, I quickly realized that I did not have the ability to turn off my feelings when the clock struck 5:00 p.m. I counseled and helped children and teenagers with drinking and drug problems. It was a horrible experience. I was exposed to a six-year-old alcoholic, a nine-year-old drug user, and a ten-year-old sexually abused child. I had a very difficult time with these situations. I became too emotionally involved, and I could not turn off my feelings. It was the most depressing six months ever. For me, witnessing the trauma that these kids went through was terrible. I felt you had to become numb to your feelings to be able to do this job.

At this time, I knew I could never be a psychologist or counselor. I was already overly sensitive and numb because of Jim and Bruce. Feeling that this environment would become more and more unhealthy for me, I decided not to pursue continuing education after my internship. I had enough problems I had to personally deal with and to heal from. Plus, I still had to try to help and heal my own family.

After college and in my twenties, I did a lot of soul searching. The last two decades have brought me major spiritual learning and exploration. The injustice of Jim's and Bruce's deaths shook even my most firmly held beliefs about religion, morality, life's meaning, and my self-belief about family and friends.

I had many sleepless nights remembering that horrible day, and I questioned all of my beliefs. I wondered for years why this had happened. What good would come out of it? Why did I survive?

These questions led me to explore and develop a deep sense of spirituality. I was trying to make sense of it all. I read *hundreds* of spiritual and self-help books. The books were fantastic. They helped me become grounded and find perspective. These books, combined with my own self-exploration, helped me to uncover and embrace a new sense of faith and understanding about my personal journey.

My love for the mountains and hiking gave me a sense of self–exploration, a place to find peace and harmony to overcome my fears and sadness. Hiking gave me a sense of resolution. I cannot explain it, but it calmed me down walking amongst the pine trees, standing on top of a high mountain ridge, looking at the deep blue sky, breathing in that fresh clean air, having the warm sun on my face and enjoying that beautiful, rugged scenery. It feels like God's country to me - like I'm closer to God. It was a place I found solitude and a place I found freedom to feel joy. Hiking provided me an avenue to find peace within myself, to think about my thoughts and feelings. It was a place that gave me joy and understanding. It provided me a sense of release, which allowed me to find my way through it all.

I never used or rationalized what had happened as an excuse to behave a certain way. I could have easily turned toward drugs and drinking, but I realized at age seventeen that life, unfortunately, throws curve balls and bad things can happen. You just have to accept it and move on. You cannot blame others, and/or use a bad situation as an excuse to not make your life better. Too many people make excuses for their problems instead of facing the facts and resolving their own issues. It is much easier to blame other people.

It's hard for me to have sympathy for people who do not take responsibility for their problems. If I can take responsibility for my problems, my sadness and my life path, so can everyone else. The way I look at it, you have two choices: One, be miserable, wallow in self pity, blame your life on all that went wrong, and be unhappy; or two, take a bad or negative situation and turn it into something good and right. Learn from your experiences and live your life to the fullest. I personally decided to do the second. I wanted to be happy, positive and successful. I did not want to be sad and negative anymore.

I decided the most important thing to do was to always take a good attitude that something positive has to come from something negative. Believing that I am here for a reason — is why I survived that day. Maybe it was to write this book; maybe to help people understand mental illness; or maybe to help people understand death and mourning. I don't know, but I do believe with all my heart that everything (good or bad) happens for a reason. I believe God does not give you things you cannot handle. Everyone has a certain spiritual journey that needs to be fulfilled or followed. I believe life is about experiences - Taking what you learn from those experiences and growing spiritually. This is what helps you learn your own strengths and develop your faith. Plus, it helps you learn what you do not want in life.

Looking back, would I change it? That is a difficult question to ask myself, because on one hand, yes, I would love to have all three of my brothers back. But on the other hand, I became a better person for it. You spiritually grow through the most negative and bad situations. So, I am very grateful for what I went through and what I have learned. This experience allowed me to help other people in regards to mental illness and dealing with death. There is nothing better in life than to help someone else.

Overall, how has the situation affected me in general? I'm not going to lie, it has affected me deeply, emotionally and physically.

Life has definitely been far from perfect. I still emotionally have a little bit of a hard time opening my heart up to people and trusting them, especially in relationships.

Over the years, I have had a few friends make comments to me that I have a wall around me, and I portray myself as closed. They often encouraged me to let the walls down and allow people to see who I really am. I have to admit, a lot of times, I don't realize that I am even doing that. I guess it's an unconscious mechanism I developed from what happened that day in the house with Jim and Bruce. When Ricky was an ever-present threat, I instinctively learned to protect myself and be on guard. So I completely understand why my friends would perceive that about me.

I've consciously tried to change; however, sometimes it is really hard. When you had someone in your life you loved, admired and adored, then they commit the ultimate betrayal, like killing family members and taking away your childhood, it's a little hard to trust again. Like many people, over the years, I have been hurt and let down by family and friends. So, with it all compounded together, I do not open up to people easily; however, once I do, I am the most loyal friend.

And yes, I still tend to be a little quiet and withdrawn at times. I think subconsciously I believe that if I get too close to people, they will leave or die. I am still afraid to open up about what has happened to my family. I am afraid that people will still pass judgment and use this information against us. Unfortunately, our culture still has prejudice and ignorance about mental illness, which makes it difficult to talk about until now. Sharing this story has released a burden of heaviness that I never realized I was carrying because it had become so much a part of me.

That day I spent in the closet, I had a "stress-induced stroke." After that day, I had difficulties with speech. I would say sentences or words backwards. I would lose my balance and stumble easily. I would get bad headaches and blurry vision. My hands would feel weak and I would have difficulties opening up bottle or jar. I also experienced memory loss of childhood events. I told the doctors for many years that something had happened to me in the closet. I described all the symptoms of a stroke, but most of the doctors ignored me and told me it was Post-Traumatic Stress Syndrome. I knew it was something more than that.

Finally, after eighteen years, my doctor was shocked to hear that no other doctor had taken the time or effort to have my brain scanned. I went through MRI tests to discover I did have a black mark on my brain. However, the doctor could not determine one hundred percent if it was damage from a stroke because it was eighteen years too late. The doctor felt it was, but we don't know for sure. I know I had a stroke. Still to this day, I have memory loss of times prior to Jim and Bruce's deaths. I lose my balance easily. I experience bad headaches, and I still have speech difficulties when I am really tired, relaxed or nervous. It's hard because I know what I'm saying in my head, but my words come out all jumbled. People tease me or correct me all the time, but I never have the guts to tell them why I speak that way. I am always afraid they will ask me why I had a stroke, which means I will have to tell them my story — and I never wanted to do that until now.

Writing this book was a way for me to make something good out of something bad. I always knew after Jim and Bruce died that I would write this book. I actually started writing fifteen years ago but never found the time, energy or heart to finish it until now. After Ricky died, I knew it was time to tell his story. I knew I had to share with people what it was like to live with a mentally ill person and what my family had endured. I knew it was time to open the closet door and let people in so I can help other families prevent the same tragedy. I hope with all my heart that in reading this book you will learn something new about mental illness; you will learn compassion; and you will reach a better understanding about the seriousness of this disease.

I called the book "Silent Voices" because I thought it was a great analogy of what Ricky, myself, my family and other mentally ill people go through. This title represents the voices like myself who cannot tell anyone what was happening at home; the voices of the parents and family who are heartbroken and can't get any doctors to listen; the voices of the mentally ill people who can't explain or express what they are going through; and most importantly, the voice of Ricky, of his story, of his illness.

Finally, on a personal note, I have to say, "Thank you" to Ricky. We shared a unique experience that will be a part of me for the rest of my life. If it were not for Ricky, I would not be the person I am today. Ricky taught me a level of spirituality that I otherwise would have never known. He taught me a level of understanding and compassion I would have never been able to find by myself. He taught me to listen, to see people for who they really are and to look into their hearts. I will always love Ricky. He will never be forgotten, and I hope everything I love about him will always continue to live inside of me.

Because of Ricky, whenever I see mentally ill people on the street, in the park, or in a store, I always say a quick, quiet little prayer for them: "God, please bless them and take care of them and their families." Next time you see a mentally ill person, please don't pass judgment or make fun of him or her. Remember my story. You have no idea what that person or their family has gone through. You do not know the pain and sorrow they have endured. Please make an effort to say a little prayer for them and please be kind.

Would You Like To Help My Cause?

With the passing of my mom, I would like to honor her dream of building a halfway house for schizophrenics in Ricky's name and memory. I too, would like to make this dream come true not only for her but for my brother. I have created Silent Voices Foundation to help support mental illness and provide a place where a percentage of the proceeds from this book will be donated. If you would like to donate to help me raise money to build a halfway house, to help support an existing mental facility, or to support research, please send your donation to my foundation listed below. I would be so grateful for your contribution! If you would like to make a donation for mental illness in your local area, please see the next chapter for some references.

Silent Voices Foundation
www.silentvoicesfoundation.org

Please visit my website for more information about my charity and my contact information.

Thank you!

In Loving Memory
Jim

A year ago today, I saw a new release
They said that you'd been shot, and that you were deceased.

Sometimes it feels like yesterday, the pain is so acute
Anger at a system, although the point is moot.

Sometimes it frightens me, because I can't recall
Your image getting softer, behind a gossamer wall.

A sensitive and gentle man – always reading books
Panoramic knowledge, from herbs to mountain brooks.

An underlying intensity, beneath the surface calm
You had indeed survived a Hell, you lived through
Viet Nam.

You lived life to the fullest, caught salmon off the coast
Believed in reincarnation, And of course the Holy Ghost.

You came back to help, a brother that you loved
Our fate or karma meets us, destined from above

All of you were victims – you and Bruce and Rick
Of overcrowded hospitals, of laws not meant to stick.

This never should have happened, all the tears and pain
The sorrow of your family, this muddy, narrow lane.

When will we learn to distribute – all our country's wealth?
Quit spending on old men's war games, instead of mental health?

When will our courts protect – the victims of the crime
When will federal spending, spare mental health a dime?

Changing the law now, will never bring you back
But maybe it will save someone, from riding down this track.

I hope your destination, past the River and the Wall
Fills you with new pleasures, like the bugling of the Elk call.

By: Our Dear Family Friend
Shellee K. Spellman
1984

In Loving Memory
Bruce

How do you like it – in your home up in the sky?
Can you look down and see us – can you hear us cry?
I hope that your death, has not been in vain
That our anguish at our loss, will give the world a gain.

I remember how your smile, could light your face aglow
And how you loved the mountains, not so long ago.
But now your body rests in the earth below
And every night I pray, please don't let it snow.

The days are getting better, but at night I find no rest
In the darkness, tears course – from my cheeks unto my chest.
Death they say is not proud, the uninvited guest
The unfairness of it all, burns in my throat and breast.

Twenty years upon this earth isn't enough time
To smell all of the flowers, to taste all of the wine.
Why is it that God picks the gentle and the kind
And leaves we more imperfect beings far, far behind.

The Irony of Violent Death upon the Gentle Soul
This is the greatest burden, it takes the greatest toll.

You should have lived a long life, been buried in a knoll
Instead shot by your brother, a tortured, frightened soul.

It makes me sick to think, your last moments in this life
Were filled with terror and confusion, pursued by gun and knife.
Knowing Jim had been shot, you ran to call for aid
Then realizing you too were pursued – in this bloody raid.

How does one beg for mercy, from one who is not sane?
While watching life pass o'er thee, the sunlight and the rain
And upstairs, they heard you, "Don't do it Rick!" you cried
The shot rang out, and in their hearts, they knew that you had died.

Your friend, she held you in her arms
And slowly watched you die
Your last words were a prayer
Now you're home up in the sky.

And God, I hope there is a heaven
That you reside up in the sky
That you're warm and safe and happy now
That my life is not a lie.

If I could know you're there, not in the cold below
Why then the winter could come, and hence then come the snow.
And somehow I can handle, the fact that you have died
If I know your shine on me, from Colorado skies.

By: Our Dear Family Friend
Shellee K. Spellman
1983

Chapter Twelve

Epilogue
Shh... Don't Say That Bad Word

S ad! Angry! These are the first words that come to my mind when I think about how many people portray mental illness as a social stigma.

What does stigma really mean? The dictionary states that stigma means: "Mark of disgrace or reproach;" or "A mark of shame or discredit."

When did illness become a disgrace? When did illness become a shame?

Unfortunately, mental illness is not considered an illness; instead it is considered a character flaw, personality issue or an annoying family problem. Shame on society for thinking this way! Shame on us for being so ignorant to think that mental illness is not disease! It is. It is a chemical imbalance in the brain. It is a physical ailment.

More than one fourth (25%) of the world population has some type of mental illness. More people have mental illness than cancer, diabetes, heart disease, Alzheimer's, MS or MD, yet we ignore it as a disease and treat it like we use to treat leprosy.

This has been a problem for hundreds of years in societies

around the world. My question is why?

It is shocking to me because we are supposed to be in an "enlightened age," yet mental illness still carries a stigma. Stigma can assume many forms, both subtle and blatant. It appears as prejudice, discrimination, fear, avoidance, distrust and stereotyping.

I find it interesting that when people talk about someone's illness - for instance, cancer, heart disease or the flu, they will discuss it openly. However, if it is mental illness, say depression or schizophrenia - they will whisper about it. Why? Are they afraid that they, too, will succumb to this disease if they admit it is real? Do they feel that they are somehow protecting the dignity of the person with the illness if they whisper rather than talk normally about a person's mental illness? Are they afraid that people will pass judgment? Bingo! That is it. People are embarrassed to speak about mental illness. I guess whispering makes it more tolerable to talk about.

I have to admit, I am somewhat guilty. When my brother came home sick, I did not tell anyone. I was not necessarily embarrassed of him per se. Rather, I was deeply hurt, sad, and wanted to help. I just did not know how to explain what was wrong with him.

As Ricky's illness progressed, I became more confused and felt resentment toward his illness. I did not understand the symptoms. So, I continued to keep it a secret. Maybe in reality I was embarrassed or ashamed. I did not know anyone else who had a family member that was sick with a mental illness. I started to think, "Why us?" and "Why Ricky?" I guess I did not trust people. I too felt they would pass judgment on the brother I loved and cared about. It was easier to keep it quiet than to share the frustrations and deal with the comments.

My poor mom dealt with the stigma against Ricky the whole

time she tried to get him help. My mom was brought up to believe that you help people in need. Most of the time, she was in shock and disbelief about the way other human beings treated her and Ricky. The very people who you'd think would help, like doctors and counselors, were the ones who turned their backs. The very people you'd think would care, like family, neighbors, close friends and church friends, were all suddenly too busy to see my mom or answer her calls. They did not want to hear about the illness or help. They wanted to ignore "it," as in Ricky and her. I don't think she ever got over those hurt feelings.

After Jim and Bruce died, my family and I experienced even more stigma against mental illness and of course, what Ricky had done. We had a family in the neighborhood that tried to start a petition to force us to move.

A neighbor lady who lived a couple blocks away (my family did not know her) actually had the nerve to say to my brother Eugene two days after Jim and Bruce died that she was glad Bruce was dead! She stated that he was a bad kid and caused trouble. She also stated that Ricky was bad, too, and my family probably deserved it. My brother was slack jawed with shock and didn't even know what to say. How could someone be so cruel! I still get extremely upset when I hear this story.

Personally, I experienced distance from kids at school. No one wanted to talk to me and I felt shunned. Some kids did not treat me kindly. They gossiped about me, they pointed their fingers at me as I walked down the hall, they the shut the door on me, and they ignored me if I said hi. It hurt me deeply and I didn't understand why. That was the only time in my life that I really felt completely embarrassed about Ricky and what he did. I feel angry with myself for allowing people to make me feel that way because I still loved Ricky. I still felt deep compassion for him.

Over the years, there were many times when my brothers and I experienced rude comments from people who knew our family. They passed judgment on what happened. They never bothered to ask us what really happened and why. They just made unfair comments about Ricky and our family. They did not want to be associated with us. I don't know why. I guess they thought if they talked to us, they might be "infected" by mental illness. Sounds crazy, but I actually think people believe that is possible.

Sometimes, I would hear people make rude comments or make fun of mentally ill people. It always rubbed me the wrong way. Do we make fun of people with cancer? Do we make fun of people with heart disease? Of course not, so why is it okay to make fun of someone who is sick with mental illness or be ashamed of it?

I also experienced stigma after I wrote this book. I was at a book event in Atlanta, Georgia. A lady came up to the table and personally told me that she could not buy my book. She told me that mental illness was the sign of the devil. She did not believe in mental illness. She stated that my family was possessed with evil because this tragedy happened. I was shocked! Was it really necessary for her to come out of her way to tell me this? With the ability we have today to educate ourselves, and all the medical proof that is available, I cannot believe there are still people out there that think like that. I just told her nicely, "Thank you. Please go be with God, because I know he was with me and is proud of me for sharing my story."

Our society, which includes you and me, needs to break down the barriers of ignorance, prejudice and discrimination against people who suffer with mental illness and their families. We need to promote education, understanding, compassion and respect.

Fifty-four million Americans are affected by mental disorders each year and these diseases do not discriminate. Wealthy, poor, educated, uneducated, urban, rural, young, old, of any race; anyone can be affected by mental illness. The chemical imbalances that cause mental illness can be inherited, or triggered by undue stress or substance abuse. These brain disorders can be just like chemical disturbance in other organs of the body, like those that cause diabetes, but instead of receiving compassion and acceptance, people with mental illness often experience hostility, discrimination and stigma.

We need to remember that people, who have illnesses and diseases, should not be defined by it. Mental illness is a physical ailment. It is a disease and we need to treat it with the respect that it deserves.

Whether you are affected by mental illness or not, please push past the misperceptions, and educate yourself with facts. One of the best ways you can help someone with mental illness is by understanding what it is, and what it isn't. After all, myths about mental illness contribute to stigma.

I hope my book will inspire conversations with your family and friends about mental illness.

Please encourage people to buy and read my book so they can learn understanding and compassion for mental illness, and what it is like for a family that cannot get help. This is my way of trying to break the "social stigma" against mental illness by making people aware of the struggles.

We must break the stigma!

One step at a time... The first step, acceptance.

CHAPTER THIRTEEN

Did You Know?

What is Schizophrenia?

Schizophrenia is a chronic, severe and disabling brain disease that interferes with normal brain and mental function. It can trigger hallucinations, delusions, paranoia and significant lack of motivation. Without treatment, schizophrenia affects the ability to think clearly, manage emotions, and interact appropriately with other people. Schizophrenia is one of the most debilitating of all mental illnesses and can profoundly affect all areas of your life.

Basic Facts:

- Schizophrenia is found all over the world — in all races, all cultures and all social classes
- Approximately 1.1 percent of the world's population develops schizophrenia
- 51 million people worldwide suffer from schizophrenia
- More than 2.7 million Americans now suffer from schizophrenia (1 in 100)
- There are more Americans with schizophrenia than there are residents of North Dakota and Wyoming combined
- For men, the age of onset for schizophrenia is often ages 16 to 20

- For women, the age of onset is sometimes later — ages 25 to 30
- Schizophrenia is rare under the age of 10
- The disease affects men and women equally
- One out of ten schizophrenics eventually commits suicide
- Studies indicate that 25 percent of those who have schizophrenia recover completely (on lifetime medication); 50 percent improve over a 10-year period; and 25 percent do not improve or recover
- Less than half receive adequate treatment, including appropriate medication dosage and use of various therapies
- There is no cure for schizophrenia. It's a brain disease with concrete and specific symptoms due to physical and biochemical changes in the brain
- In America, schizophrenia cases relative to other diseases: schizophrenia, 2.7 million; Alzheimer's disease, 1.3 million people; multiple sclerosis, 400,000 people; insulin-dependent diabetes, 350,000 people; and muscular dystrophy, 35,000 people
- Schizophrenia receives less money from the government and charities for studies for a cure than any other disease, but yet it has one of the highest disease rates

What Causes Schizophrenia?

Scientists do not know for sure what causes schizophrenia. It is believed there is no single cause of this illness. Some researchers believe that schizophrenia can be a result of many factors such as genetic predisposition, biochemistry (neuro-chemical imbalance in the brain), environmental exposures and/or stresses during pregnancy or childhood, cerebral blood flow (activity between different areas of the brain), molecular biology (irregular pattern of certain brain cells), drug abuse and nutrition.

What are the Symptoms?

The symptoms of schizophrenia usually emerge in adolescence or early adulthood. Symptoms can appear suddenly or may develop gradually, often causing the illness to go unrecognized and untreated until it is in an advanced stage when it is more difficult to treat.

The symptoms are not identical for everyone. Some people may have only one episode of schizophrenia in their lifetime. Others may have recurring episodes, but lead relatively normal lives in between. Others may have severe symptoms for a lifetime.

The symptoms of schizophrenia can be divided into five basic categories: Psychotic, Negative, Cognitive Impairment, Mood Problems and Behavioral Disturbances. No two people are alike. Every schizophrenic is unique and will display signs of these symptoms to different degrees in most of these categories, but no one has all of the symptoms in each category.

Psychotic Symptoms:
- Perceptions or beliefs that reflect a break from reality
- Absurd or false thoughts, behaviors or feelings
- These symptoms can fluctuate over time
- Hallucinations — false perceptions — and sensations that the person experiences but other people do not. These perceptions include hearing, seeing, feeling, tasting and smelling things that are not present in the environment.
- Delusions — a false belief — which appear quite real to the person but seem impossible or untrue to others. Examples:
  » Persecutory Delusions — a person believes he is being persecuted unfairly or that people want to harm him for no good reason. (FBI conspiring to kill him or her; family secretly poisoning his or her food; people are working together to drive him or her crazy.)
  » Delusions of Reference — mistaken belief that

something or someone is sending a message or referring to the person with schizophrenia. (The person may believe that TV, radio or newspaper has a special message for him or her. Things in their environment like objects, letters or numbers may be interpreted as conveying a symbolic message.)

» Delusion of Control — involves the belief that another person or force can control the person's thoughts or actions (other people can put thoughts into his or her head or take away his or her thoughts).

» Grandiose Delusions — the belief that they are special, have unique talents or are rich (e.g., they invented the Boeing 747. They are an unrecognized artistic genius).

Negative Symptoms:

- Absence of normal thoughts, behaviors or feelings
- These symptoms can be fairly stable over time
- Blunted Affect — noticeable lack of expression of emotion (decreased facial and vocal expressiveness — they talk about something humorous or sad without showing any amusement or sadness in their facial expression or tone of voice).
- Alogia — psychological term for saying very little (not conveying much in speech — it's difficult keeping a conversation going).
- Apathy — does not feel motivated to work toward personal goals or function more independently (apathy reflects discouragement and hopelessness about the future — lack of motivation can also interfere with even the most basic tasks, such as daily hygiene and excessive sleep in order to avoid others).
- Anhedonia — decreased ability to feel pleasure or enjoyment (reading, watching a movie, playing a game, or talking with other people my no longer make them feel good).

Cognitive Impairment:

- Problems with cognition (thought processes) — interferes with basic activities such as having conversations with others, going to work or school, and self-care.
- Basic Cognitive Functions — different problems in processing information:
  - » Problems or difficulties with attention and concentration — easily distracted
  - » Decreased psychomotor speed — takes longer to process information and respond accordingly
  - » Memory problems
  - » Troubles with executive functioning — the ability to perform complex tasks that may require abstract reasoning, planning and problem solving — for example, they can't manage money or handle conflict
- Social Perception — lack of ability to recognize and understand important signals that occur during interactions with others — they can't get another person's perspective and lack empathy
- Language Problems — difficulties with thinking are immediately evident when a person uses language in an odd way that is hard to understand — they may jump from one topic to another or use remotely related topics — stop in the middle of a sentence — make up new words
- Poor Insight — lack insight into the fact that they have a psychiatric illness — they believe nothing is wrong with them

Mood Problems:

- Mood problems can be long-standing or temporary — depression and suicidal tendencies, anxiety, anger, hostility, suspiciousness and inappropriate behavior
- They have feelings of hopelessness, helplessness and worthlessness

- Belief that others want to hurt them — scared to be in a social environment
- Can have a short fuse — they are easily angered or consistently hostile or suspicious — making them difficult to get along with
- Mood may fluctuate rapidly from happy to sad or angry, for no apparent reason
- Smiling or laughing when talking about a serious topic, such as the death of a friend or family member

Behavioral Disturbances:

- Catatonia and Mustim behaviors can be rare in schizophrenia — Catatonia is the state in which the person maintains the same body posture many hours and days — he or she may be in a stupor, dazed and unable to engage in any purposeful behavior. Mustim — refusing to talk

Quick Reference Warning Signs:
(these differ from person to person):

- Social withdrawal, isolation, and reclusiveness
- Deterioration of personal hygiene
- Depression
- Bizarre behavior
- Irrational statements
- Sleeping excessively or inability to sleep
- Shift in basic personality
- Unexpected hostility
- Deterioration of social relationships
- Hyperactivity or inactivity — or alternating between the two
- Inability to concentrate or to cope with minor problems
- Extreme preoccupation with religion or with the occult
- Excessive writing without meaning
- Indifference
- Dropping out of activities — or out of life in general

- Decline in academic or athletic interests
- Forgetting things
- Losing possessions
- Extreme reactions to criticism
- Inability to express joy
- Inability to cry or excessive crying
- Inappropriate laughter
- Unusual sensitivity to stimuli (noise, light, colors, textures)
- Attempts to escape through frequent moves or hitchhiking trips
- Drug or alcohol abuse
- Fainting
- Strange posturing
- Refusal to touch persons or objects; wearing gloves, etc.
- Shaving head or body hair
- Cutting oneself; threats of self-mutilation
- Staring without blinking — or blinking incessantly
- Flat, reptile-like gaze
- Rigid stubbornness
- Peculiar use of words or odd language structures
- Sensitivity and irritability when touched by others

How is a Schizophrenia Diagnosed?

There is no laboratory test that has been found to be diagnostic of schizophrenia. The disease has been primarily diagnosed with family and personal medical history, physical examination, and a mental health assessment. Other tests, such as blood tests or imaging tests, may be done to rule out other illnesses (such as a major depressive episode or a manic episode with psychotic features, delusional disorder, autistic disorder, personality disorders) that can mimic symptoms of schizophrenia. It is important to analyze the symptoms for consecutive months prior to determining if someone has schizophrenia. There are also other medical tests or options that can be taken, such as brain-imaging (brain scans). There have been many studies done that show individuals with schizophrenia often have a number of (non-diagnostic) neurological abnormalities. They have enlargement of lateral ventricles, decreased brain tissue, decreased volume of the temporal lobe and thalamus, a large cavum septum pellucidi and hypofrontality (decreased blood flow and metabolic functioning of the frontal lobes).

Personally, I cannot tell you who is schizophrenic and who is not. I have no medical degree. I can state that my brother exhibited most of the warning signs, and his brain scan did show some abnormalities. I just wish that all this information had existed when my parents were educating themselves on this illness and searching for help. Overall, it is best to speak with your doctor about all the symptoms you have observed, review family medical history, and also ask about other options for testing prior to determining if your loved one has schizophrenia.

What are the Treatments for Schizophrenia?
There is no cure for schizophrenia, however, it is a treatable disease. The last few years have seen dramatic steps forward in the treatment of schizophrenia. Between new medications, enhanced prescribing knowledge, and new knowledge demonstrating effective psychosocial treatments, we now have a greatly improved understanding of how to treat the biological, psychological and social aspects of a person's illness. These available options are making recovery a very real possibility for all individuals who have schizophrenia.

It is important to diagnose and treat schizophrenia as early as possible to have success in the treatment plan. Schizophrenia is a difficult disease to handle for both the individual who is sick and for his or her family. It is critical to have consistency, long-term treatment of medications, and emotional support to have any type of success in the management of this disease.

In General — Mental Illness:

I felt it was important to touch base on the general statistics about mental illness. Schizophrenia is not the only difficult mental disease that is affecting millions of families. The statistics are alarming.

- According to the World Health Organization, one in every four people, or 25 percent of individuals, develops one or more mental disorders at some stage in their lives.
- Today, 450 million people globally suffer from mental disorders in both developed and developing countries.
- Of these, 154 million suffer from depression, 25 million from Schizophrenia, 91 million from alcohol-use disorder and 15 million from drug-use disorder.
- Mental illnesses are more common than cancer, diabetes or heart disease.
- As many as two-thirds of all people with a diagnosable mental disorder do not seek treatment, whether for fear of being stigmatized, fear that the treatment may be worse than the illness itself, or lack of awareness, access and affordability of care.
- Mental health problems represent five out of 10 leading causes of disability worldwide, amounting to nearly one-third of the disabilities in the world. Leading contributors include depression, bipolar disorder, schizophrenia, substance abuse and dementia.
- Mental illness ranks first among the illnesses that cause disability in the United States, Canada and Western Europe.
- It is predicted that in 2014, depression will be the leading cause of disability worldwide, not cancer, heart disease, diabetes, or AIDS.

- Mental illness is a serious public health challenge that is under-recognized as a public burden. It is the most ignored disease.
- Suicide claims a life every 30 seconds — almost 3,000 people commit suicide every day in this world.
- In 90 percent of suicides, mental illness is the attributing cause.
- Approximately 20.9 million American adults ages 18 and older have a mood disorder (Depression, Dysthmia and Bipolar) — that is 9.5 percent of the U.S. population.
- Approximately 40 million American adults ages 18 and older have an anxiety disorder (Panic, Obsessive-Compulsive, Post-Traumatic Stress, Anxiety and Social Phobia) — that is 18.1% of the U.S. population.
- Nearly 500,000 mentally ill men and women are serving time in U.S. jails and prisons.
- Approximately 40 percent of people who are homeless in America suffer from serious and persistent mental illness.

Educate Yourself:

The best advice I can give is to educate yourself about schizophrenia or mental illness disorders. Make yourself aware of all the symptoms so you will be able to handle your situation to the best of your abilities. Today, there is so much information available by Internet, books, magazines and support groups. When I did the research for this chapter, I was amazed and excited to see how much information was out there. None of this information existed when my brother was sick. There were not many books, only a few magazine articles, no Internet access, and there were no support groups. With the large amount of people who deal with some type of mental illness, there are fabulous resources available.

This would be my suggestion regarding what to do if you have or suspect someone in your family is mentally ill.

- Take initiative and educate yourself — research as much as possible (Internet, books, magazines, etc.).

- Ask a lot of questions of your doctor about the illness: signs and symptoms, expected course of the illness, medication and treatment strategies, signs of possible relapse and other related information.
- Be persistent — find a doctor who is familiar with Schizophrenia or the mental disorder you are dealing with.
- Assist the doctor/psychiatrist — tell them what you have observed — supply as much information as possible — be specific.
- Participate in family counseling.
- Research residential and rehabilitation programs.
- Research family education programs.
- Research self-help groups or supporting groups.
- Be positive and supportive.
- Learn how to cope with stress together.
- And most importantly, be good to yourself.

Resources:

In researching this chapter for facts and figures, everything I wrote was taken from the below resources. I am also going to list extra resources that I found to help provide information that would be beneficial in helping your family's journey of understanding and coping with mental illness. Finally, I hope with all my heart that my story and the facts that I provided help you to understand mental illness a little more today than you did yesterday.

Organizations:

The National Alliance on Mental Illness (NAMI)
  3803 N Fairfax Drive, Suite 100
  Arlington, VA 22203
  Phone: 703-5274-7600
  Helpline: 1-800-950-NAMI (6264)
  Website: http://www.nami.org

National Mental Health Association (NMHA) now Mental Health
of America
>   2000 N Beauregard Street, 6th Floor
>   Alexandria, VA 22311
>   Phone: 703-684-7722 or 1-800-969-6642
>   Helpline: 1-800-273-TALK (8255)
>   Website: http://www.nmha.org

National Mental Health Consumers' Self-Help Clearinghouse
>   1211 Chestnut Street, Suite 1000
>   Philadelphia, PA 19107
>   Phone: 1-800-553-4539 or 215-751-1810
>   Website: http://mhselfhelp.org

National Alliance for Research on Schizophrenia and Depression
(NARSAD)
>   60 Cutter Mill Road, Suite 404
>   Great Neck, NY 11021
>   Phone: 516-829-0091
>   InfoLine:1-800-829-8289
>   Website: http://narsad.org

National Institute of Mental Health (NIMH)
Science Writing, Press and Dissemination Branch
>   6001 Executive Boulevard, Room 8184, MSC 9663
>   Bethesda, MD 20892-9663
>   Phone: 301-443-4513
>   Toll-free: 1-866-615-6464
>   Email: nimhinfo@nih.gov
>   Website: http://nimh.nih.gov

The Menninger Clinic
    2801 Gessner Drive
    Houston, TX 77080
    Phone: 713-275-5000
    Toll-free: 1-800-351-9058
    Website: www.menningerclinic.com

ASHA International (A Source of Hope for All touched by Mental Illness)
    2969 NW 127th Avenue
    Portland, OR 97229
    Phone: 971-340-7190
    Website: www.myasha.org

The Center for Reintegration, Inc.
    350A West 49th Street
    New York, NY 10019
    Phone: 212-957-9050
    Website: www.reintegration.com

American Psychological Association
    750 First Street NE
    Washington, DC 2002-4242
    Phone: 800-374-2721 or 202-336-5500
    Website: www.apa.org

American Psychiatric Association
    1000 Wilson Boulevard, Suite 1825
    Arlington, VA 22209
    Phone: 1-888-35-PSYCH or 1-888-35-77924
    Website: www.psych.org

National Association of Social Workers
    750 First Street, NE Suite 700
    Washington, DC 20002-7241
    Phone: 1-800-742-4089
    Website: http://socialworkers.org

Internet Websites:
http://Schizophrenia.com
www.medicinenet.com/Schizophrenia/article.htm
www.webmd.com/Schizophrenia/default.htm
www.mayoclinic.com/health/Schizophrenia/DS00196
www.mentalhealth.com
www.answers.com/topic/Schizophrenia
www.health.yahoo.net
www.menningerclinic.com
http://www.nami.org
http://www.nmha.org
http://mhselfhelp.org
http://narsad.org
http://nimh.nih.gov
www.psychologyinfo.com/Schizophrenia/support.htm
www.mdjunction.com/ (support groups)
www.myasha.org
www.apa.org
www.psych.org
www.workplacementalhealth.org
www.Schizophreniadigest.com
www.treatmentadvocacycenter.org
www.geodon.com/
http://socialworkers.org
www.mentalhealth.org
www.reintegration.com
www.miepvideo.org
www.hearing-voices.org

Magazines:

The Advocate — NAMI's quarterly newsmagazine

Mental Health Works — a free quarterly publication focused on mental health in the workplace, www.workplacementalhealth.org

Schizophrenia Digest — www.Schizophreniadigest.com

Schizophrenia Bulletin — Schizophreniabulletin.oxfordjournals.org/

Books:

Guide for Siblings, Offspring and Parents
    by D. T. Marsh and R. Dickens

How to Cope with Mental Illness in Your Family: A Self-Care I am Not Sick, I Don't Need Help
    by Xavier Amador

My Mother's Keeper: A Daughter's Memoir of Growing Up in the Shadow of Mental Illness
    by T.E. Holly and J. Holly

Nothing to Hide: Mental Illness in the Family
    by J. Beard and P.N. Gillespie

Schizophrenia Revealed
    by M.F. Green

Surviving Schizophrenia — A Manual for Families, Patients and Providers
    by E. Fuller Torrety

Tell Me I'm Here: One Family's Experience of Schizophrenia
    by A. Deveson

The Complete Family Guide to Schizophrenia
    by Kim T. Mueser and Susan Gingerich

The Inner World of Mental Illness
    by B. Kaplan

Understanding Schizophrenia: A Guide to the New Research on Causes and Treatments
    by R.S.E. Keefe and P.D. Harvey

About
Debbie Nau Redmond

D ebbie was born and raised in Littleton, Colorado. Growing up in a family of eight children, Debbie was the youngest and developed a true understanding of family dynamics.

She always knew in her heart that her life path would lead her down a road to write a book about dealing with family tragedy. Her desire to make a difference, learn from experiences, and help other people is what motivated her to write the book *Silent Voices.*

She is currently writing her second book about working through the grieving process.

Debbie recently started a non-profit charity called *Silent Voices Foundation* to help raise money for mental illness facilities, programs and research. For more information: www.silentvoicesfoundation.org.

Debbie received her Bachelor of Arts Degree in Psychology from the University of Northern Colorado and continued her education with Business Development and Project Management certificates. She has been working in the corporate world for 25 years.

Debbie still lives in the Denver area with her husband and enjoys all the Colorado outdoor activities, such as hiking, camping, jeeping, skiing and snowshoeing. Her desire and love for the outdoors is what brings her peace and harmony.